SETTLEMENT, INDUSTRY and RITUAL

Settlement, Industry and Ritual

Proceedings of a public seminar on archaeological discoveries
on national road schemes, September 2005

Edited by Jerry O'Sullivan and Michael Stanley

Published by the National Roads Authority 2006
St Martin's House
Waterloo Road
Dublin 4

Cover illustrations
Main picture:
Reconstruction of a large farming settlement at Raystown, Co. Meath, c. AD 900 (Simon Dick for CRDS Ltd)
Smaller pictures (from left to right):
Extract from 1840 estate map showing children's burial ground at Tonybaun, Co. Mayo (courtesy of Alan Moloney, Mount Falcon)
Stone axehead from a Neolithic house at Monanny, Co. Monaghan (Claire Phelan)
Excavation of an infant skeleton at Tonybaun, Co. Mayo (courtesy of Chris Randolph)

Cover design: Wordwell Ltd

ISBN 0-9545955-2-1
ISSN 1649-3540

British Library Cataloguing-in-Publication Data.
A catalogue record for this book is available from the British Library.

First published in 2006

Typeset in Ireland by Wordwell Ltd

Printed by Castuera, Pamplona

Contents

Foreword   vii

Acknowledgements   viii

Archaeology and roads: an historic opportunity   1
Dáire O'Rourke
Senior Archaeologist, National Roads Authority

Neolithic Monanny, County Monaghan   7
Fintan Walsh
Excavation Director, Irish Archaeological Consultancy Ltd

Excavation of an early medieval vertical watermill at Killoteran, County Waterford   19
Donald Murphy and Stuart Rathbone
Excavation Directors, Archaeological Consultancy Services Ltd

Archaeological discoveries on a new section of the N2 in Counties Meath and Dublin   29
Maria FitzGerald
Project Archaeologist, Meath County Council National Roads Design Office

Excavation of a ringfort at Leggetsrath West, County Kilkenny   43
Anne-Marie Lennon
Excavation Director, Archaeological Consultancy Services Ltd

Archaeological investigation of a souterrain at Tateetra, Dundalk, County Louth   53
Avril Hayes
Excavation Director, Aegis Archaeology Ltd

Excavation of an early medieval 'plectrum-shaped' enclosure at Newtown, County Limerick   63
Frank Coyne
Excavation Director, Aegis Archaeology Ltd

Through the mill—excavation of an early medieval settlement at Raystown, County Meath   73
Matthew Seaver
Excavation Director, Cultural Resource Development Services Ltd

Excavation of a children's burial ground at Tonybaun, Ballina, County Mayo   89
Joanna Nolan
Excavation Director, Mayo County Council

Archaeological aerial survey—a bird's-eye view of the M7/M8 in County Laois   103
Lisa Courtney
Senior Archaeologist, Margaret Gowen & Co. Ltd

Death, decay and reconstruction: the archaeology of Ballykilmore cemetery, 115
County Westmeath
    John Channing and Patrick Randolph-Quinney
    Excavation Director and Osteoarchaeologist, Valerie J Keeley Ltd

Appendix 1—Radiocarbon dates from excavated archaeological sites described 129
in these proceedings

References 137

Seminar programme 141

Glossary 143

Directory of NRA Archaeologists and local authority Project Archaeologists 149

Foreword

Settlement, Industry and Ritual is the third monograph in the National Roads Authority's (NRA) archaeology monograph series and presents the proceedings of a one-day seminar for the public held at the Gresham Hotel, Dublin, on 15 September 2005. Such seminars have become a successful annual event and the papers that emanate from them form a very important part of the Archaeology Section's role in communicating the results of archaeological work undertaken on national road schemes.

Monograph No. 3 deals with a variety of interesting archaeological sites uncovered during the development of the national roads programme since 2001, in addition to offering overviews of the archaeology discovered on specific road schemes. The papers describe the discovery of previously undocumented sites and new site types, including the first Neolithic settlement identified in County Monaghan and an early medieval 'plectrum-shaped' enclosure in County Limerick. Newly identified sites from Counties Dublin, Kilkenny, Laois, Louth, Mayo, Meath, Waterford and Westmeath also feature. These discoveries, and others, demonstrate that there was a greater social diversity and complexity in Ireland's past than was previously understood. The archaeological discoveries outlined in this volume clearly reveal the potential of archaeological works connected with the road-building programme to alter our perception and understanding of our past.

The publication of this monograph amply demonstrates the Authority's commitment to publishing the results of NRA-funded archaeological investigations in a timely fashion and in a format that is readily accessible to the general reader. Over the next 12 months, in addition to publishing the proceedings of the 2006 seminar, the NRA will begin publishing a new series of monographs dealing exclusively with the archaeology discovered on specific road schemes, for example, the M4 Kilcock–Enfield–Kinnegad Motorway scheme and the N4 Sligo Inner Relief Road. Furthermore, the Archaeology Section has commissioned a feasibility study to ascertain the status of all pre-2001 archaeological reports with a view to publishing the results of earlier excavations undertaken on behalf of the NRA.

Transport 21, the current transport investment plan, reflects the Government's commitment to delivering the transport network that the country deserves and requires; as such, the national road-building programme will continue apace. The Authority's archaeological policy will ensure that the archaeological component of the road-building programme is well resourced and carried out efficiently and according to best practice. More importantly, the Authority will continue to bring the results of this archaeological work to the attention of the wider public through the present monograph series and a range of other media.

Fred Barry
Chief Executive
National Roads Authority

Acknowledgements

The NRA would like to express its appreciation to John Channing, Lisa Courtney, Frank Coyne, Maria FitzGerald, Avril Hayes, Anne-Marie Lennon, Donald Murphy, Joanna Nolan, Dáire O'Rourke, Patrick Randolph-Quinney, Stuart Rathbone, Matthew Seaver and Fintan Walsh for their contributions to the seminar and proceedings. The 2005 seminar was organised by Róisín Barton-Murray, archaeologist, NRA. Sarah Breslin and Anneliese Jones, NRA, Michael MacDonagh, project archaeologist, and Gráinne Leamy, assistant project archaeologist, Donegal County Council National Roads Design Office and Elspeth Logan, assistant project archaeologist, Kildare County Council National Roads Design Office also assisted in the organisation of the seminar on the day.

Jerry O'Sullivan, project archaeologist, Galway County Council National Roads Design Office, and Michael Stanley, assistant archaeologist, NRA, prepared the proceedings for publication. Gráinne Leamy and Michael Stanley compiled the glossary. Aegis Archaeology Ltd, Archaeological Consultancy Services Ltd, Cultural Resource Development Services Ltd, Irish Archaeological Consultancy Ltd, Margaret Gowen & Co. Ltd, Mayo County Council and Valerie J Keeley Ltd all kindly supplied illustrations from their recent work on national road schemes. Chris McWilliams and Michael Stanley, NRA, provided additional cartography. The monograph was copy-edited, designed and typeset by Wordwell Ltd.

Material from Ordnance Survey Ireland is reproduced with the permission of the Government of Ireland and Ordnance Survey Ireland under permit number EN0045206.

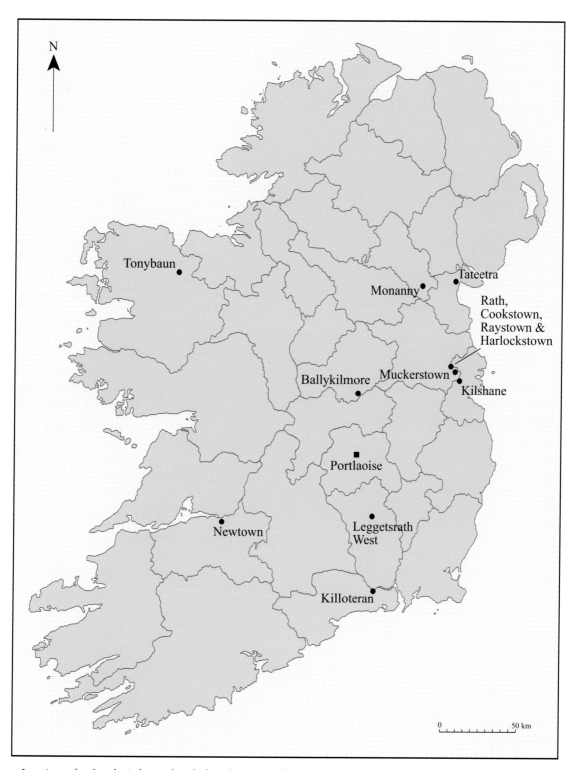

N

Tonybaun ●

Tateetra ●

Monanny ●

Rath,
Cookstown,
Raystown &
Harlockstown

Ballykilmore ●
Muckerstown ●

Kilshane ●

■ Portlaoise

Newtown ●

Leggetsrath
West ●

Killoteran ●

0　　　　　　50 km

Locations of archaeological sites described in these proceedings, showing relevant rural townland (circle) or nearest town (square).

1. Archaeology and roads: an historic opportunity
Dáire O'Rourke

Past circumstances

In the six years since a *Code of Practice* was signed by the National Roads Authority (NRA) and the Minister for Arts, Heritage, Gaeltacht and the Islands (2000), a major change has occurred in the way archaeology is considered. Prior to the *Code of Practice* and the employment of archaeologists in the NRA and local authorities there was an unstructured and inconsistent approach to archaeology on national road schemes. The NRA had no archaeological policy. While the State's policy of avoidance of known archaeological sites was acknowledged and enforced, where applicable, there was little or no appreciation of the wider archaeological landscape during the planning stages. The concept of the importance of individual sites in their setting was not recognised or addressed. This led to difficulties not only in the planning process but also later, out in the field. Few attempts were made to discern the archaeological potential of specific landscapes. There was little or no advance testing or resolution of archaeological sites. Previously unknown archaeological sites were almost exclusively uncovered during monitoring of the construction phase.

Competitive tendering for archaeological work on road schemes was rare and impracticable. The relative dearth of information at the planning stage and the lack of a considered programme in relation to archaeology meant that the projected costs were unrealistic and were not based on any attempt to assess the archaeological potential. Insufficient time and resources were allocated for archaeology. This led to major and costly delays to the roads programme, poor resourcing in relation to archaeology, and little follow-up as regards post-excavation costs and standards. The result was a poor end-product and a lack of publication.

Present developments

Planning
In Ireland's mainly agricultural economy the absence of large-scale development outside of urban areas has led to the preservation of buried remains of many tens of thousands of archaeological sites and monuments. There are over 170,000 recorded monuments throughout the country, and it is generally recognised that many more archaeological sites lie hidden beneath the soil. Modern farming practices have a significant impact on the archaeological heritage, however. The incremental erosion of archaeological features by agriculture continues largely unchecked. Major infrastructure developers such as the NRA have a significant impact on the archaeological landscape, but structures and resources are now in place to harness the archaeological resource in a proactive and efficient manner. It is now the archaeological policy of the NRA to examine the landscape affected by road constructon thoroughly during the post-planning phase but in advance of construction.

In 2006, an important objective of the NRA is to address archaeological investigation and excavation requirements to the greatest extent possible in the window of opportunity between identification of the selected route/preparation of the Environmental Impact

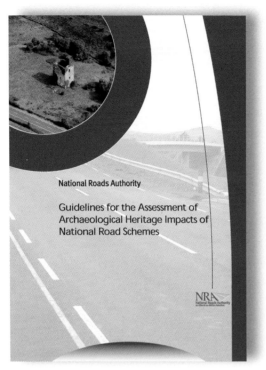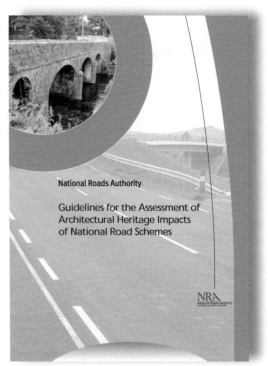

Illus. 1—The recently published (2005) archaeology and architecture planning guidelines, which form part of the NRA's environmental planning guidelines

Statement, and the scheduled arrival of the road construction contractor on site. Concentrating archaeological activity in this period has made it possible to ensure that the required human and time resources are in place to carry out the work in an efficient and effective manner and that the potential for conflict between the archaeologist and the developer is minimised. It is crucial that the on-site archaeological activities are organised and supervised so as to make maximum use of the period prior to the commencement of road construction.

Guidelines

The national road-building programme continues to have a serious impact on Ireland's archaeological heritage. It is incumbent on the NRA to manage this impact in an appropriate and responsible manner, in line with best-practice procedures and legislative/regulatory requirements. To ensure that the highest archaeological standards are met during the planning process, the NRA recently launched *Guidelines for the Assessment of Archaeological Heritage Impacts of National Road Schemes* (2005a) and *Guidelines for the Assessment of Architectural Heritage Impacts of National Road Schemes* (2005b). The aim of these publications is to provide guidance on the treatment of the archaeological and architectural heritage during the planning and design of national road schemes.

Wetland archaeology has also recently been addressed. The *Guidelines for the Testing and Mitigation of the Wetland Archaeological Heritage for National Road Schemes* (2005c) are intended to assist the project design team, project archaeologist, archaeological consultants and contractors working on testing, field survey, excavation and post-excavation phases of archaeological mitigation in wetlands on national road schemes.

Illus. 2—The wetland archaeology guidelines (2005), which form part of the NRA's environmental construction guidelines

These documents form part of a suite entitled *Environmental Assessment and Construction Guidelines*, which deal with the myriad of environmental impacts caused by major road development. It is also proposed to issue new guidelines this year in relation to the use of archaeo-geophysics on road schemes. It is hoped that all these guidelines will promote a standardised approach to the production of comprehensive reports that employ all available sources.

Legislation

The National Monuments (Amendment) Act 2004 has effected a change in procedures between the NRA and the National Monuments Section of the Department of the Environment, Heritage and Local Government. Archaeological licences are no longer required on road schemes that have received An Bord Pleanála approval; instead, the project archaeologist, on behalf of the road authority, must apply for directions in relation to archaeological work from the Minister for the Environment, Heritage and Local Government. While the Act still does not deal with the issue of what constitutes a 'National Monument', it does give the Minister discretionary powers in relation to National Monuments. If the Minister determines that a site is a National Monument, procedures are now in place either to move the road at that location or to excavate the site. However, the consolidation of the National Monuments Acts and subsequent amendments to achieve this still seem a long way off.

Research

Work is continuing on a number of research projects initiated by the NRA and relevant local authorities. The M3 Archaeology Research Framework has been implemented, under the supervision of the project archaeologist with Meath County Council, and a number of

Illus. 3—One of 1,272 skeletons from a medieval cemetery at Ballyhanna, Co. Donegal, discovered along the route of the N15 Ballyshannon–Bundoran road scheme. (Irish Archaeological Consultancy Ltd)

independent academics have been retained to assist with the archaeological, historical and palaeoenvironmental aspects of the scheme. A Newman Post-Doctoral Fellowship in Landscape Archaeology in University College Dublin is being funded by the NRA and should start delivering results in 2007. The focus of this research is twofold. On the one hand it assesses the archaeological testing techniques being carried out on national road schemes, and on the other it examines how the archaeological information from a number of specific schemes has augmented the archaeological record in those areas. This is a very exciting project as it deals with the interface of archaeological investigation techniques and information retrieval (i.e. how that information, once found, is processed). Finally, the Ballyhanna Bones Project is also a new departure for the NRA. Excavations along the N15 Ballyshannon–Bundoran road scheme revealed a medieval cemetery with 1,272 skeletons (Illus. 3). Rather than conducting a standard post-excavation study and report, the project archaeologist with Donegal County Council proposed working with third-level institutions in the north-east and north-west to develop a research agenda. A joint initiative between the NRA, Donegal County Council, Queen's University, Belfast, and the Institute of Technology, Sligo, has been developed and approved to examine the skeletal assemblage thoroughly. The various studies will include an MSc in Biomolecular Archaeology, an MSc in Archaeological Chemistry and a PhD in Osteoarchaeology. Work is due to commence on these various projects in late 2006.

The future

Outlined above is a snapshot of the innovative and expansive developments in the archaeology of national road schemes in recent months. In November 2005, the Government announced a new transport initiative—Transport 21. Following completion of the main inter-city routes, road development will concentrate on the other national primary routes, together with some work on the national secondary roads. Thus the unprecedented level of road development is set to continue.

The project archaeologists have become important elements of the National Regional Design Offices, hosted by 12 local authorities with funding by the NRA and, in most cases, integral members of the Road Design Teams. Their presence has added greatly to the quality of the archaeological aspects of the roads programme. The recent delivery of road schemes has been enabled in part by the efficient management of the archaeological resource, and by the significant pre-construction archaeological investigations carried out by consultant archaeologists under the supervision of NRA/local authority project archaeologists. It is imperative that private and public sector archaeologists continue to work together and that the skills base generated by the current work climate is maintained and, indeed, augmented.

As regards the work undertaken to date, it is planned that a number of road schemes will be published by late 2006/early 2007. Dissemination of information continues through websites, lectures, seminars, posters, brochures and media interviews. A feasibility study is currently being carried out on the status of archaeological reports resulting from work carried out on NRA road schemes from 1993 to 2001. A decision will then have to be made on what can be done and what needs to be done with this material. It is hoped that the study will highlight the gaps in the record as regards uncompleted excavation reports and unpublished significant archaeological discoveries.

Challenges

There are many challenges ahead for Irish archaeology. The archaeological work being carried out in Ireland is largely development-led, and this will continue for the foreseeable future. The ongoing pace of development, whether private or public sector, continues to put archaeological resources under pressure. For the first time in Irish archaeology, finance is not the issue. Money is in place to carry out the work but there is a shortage of people and of time. There are not enough field archaeologists, site directors, finds specialists, conservators, illustrators and managers. The profession is stretched to capacity. The work keeps coming and the post-excavation work and dissemination of results are struggling to keep up. Post-excavation work put on the long finger may never get finished. Under these conditions one must look to different methods of disseminating information—public seminars, seminars for the profession, brochures, posters, websites, magazines—to augment the traditional style of publication.

Ironically, this time of economic boom does not see a united profession. The archaeological profession has not sought to embrace this economic prosperity and to work together for the benefit of archaeology. Such benefits might include the advancement of knowledge creation through the development of national and regional archaeological strategies and research agendas, publication policies, improved field methodologies or investment in continuing professional development. While consensus may never exist in relation to archaeological thinking, there has been little attempt to keep the public abreast of the many facets of archaeological debate.

For many in the profession, the lack of publication is the main challenge facing Irish archaeology. In my view, however, the main challenge for Irish archaeology is Irish archaeologists. We have not sought to co-operate to do the best we can for our heritage or our profession. We, as a profession, have no big plan. The Foresight Study initiated in 2004 by the School of Archaeology, University College Dublin, is innovative and unique in attempting to determine where archaeology will be in 14 years time (Cooney et al. 2006). It has attempted to identify the main challenges facing the profession in the years ahead. Perhaps this study is the first step to developing this plan or vision for the future.

However, the world will not stand still. Development is ongoing in our cash-rich society. The NRA will continue to oversee the building of new roads and we will continue to carry out our archaeological work. We will continue to broaden our brief in relation to archaeological excavation and post-excavation work. We will continue to work with the State institutions and the universities. If only we can work together to satisfy clearly defined research agendas which facilitate development-led archaeology then maybe we are on the right road. We inhabit a small island that happens to be undertaking major development on the back of an economic boom. It is not going to last forever. Will future generations thank us if we squander this opportunity to maximise the benefits for our heritage and our profession?

2. Neolithic Monanny, County Monaghan

Fintan Walsh

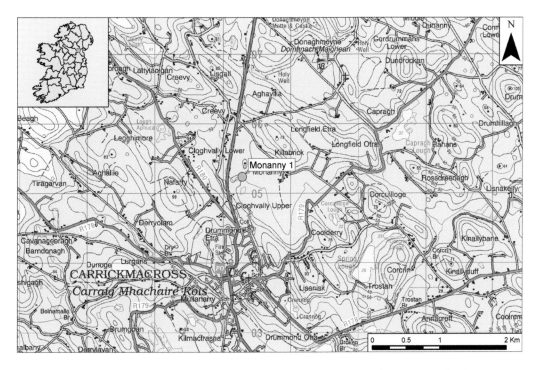

Illus. 1—Location map of Monanny, Co. Monaghan (based on the Ordnance Survey Ireland map)

The construction of the N2 Carrickmacross Bypass provided a great opportunity to investigate the previously unknown archaeological resource of this part of County Monaghan. Nestled between a low drumlin to the north and a small river and large rocky outcrop to the south; a Neolithic settlement site remained hidden in Monanny townland for nearly 6,000 years (Illus. 1).

The surrounding topography provided a sheltered location in the landscape, and this was evidently a very attractive spot for early settlers. In addition to this, the adjacent Longfield River is rich in salmon, trout and eel, and there is every reason to expect that these fish species have occupied this stretch of river for many thousands of years.

The archaeological excavation of the site was undertaken in the summer of 2003 by Irish Archaeological Consultancy Ltd on behalf of Monaghan County Council and the National Roads Authority (NGR 284280, 305240; height 37.5 m OD; excavation licence no. 03E0888). A number of distinct phases of activity were identified at Monanny: three Neolithic houses and associated pits and hearths; Bronze Age activity in the form of a burnt mound and pits; an early medieval cereal-drying kiln; a medieval burial; and post-medieval agricultural features (Illus. 2 & 3). This paper concentrates on the Neolithic phase of activity.

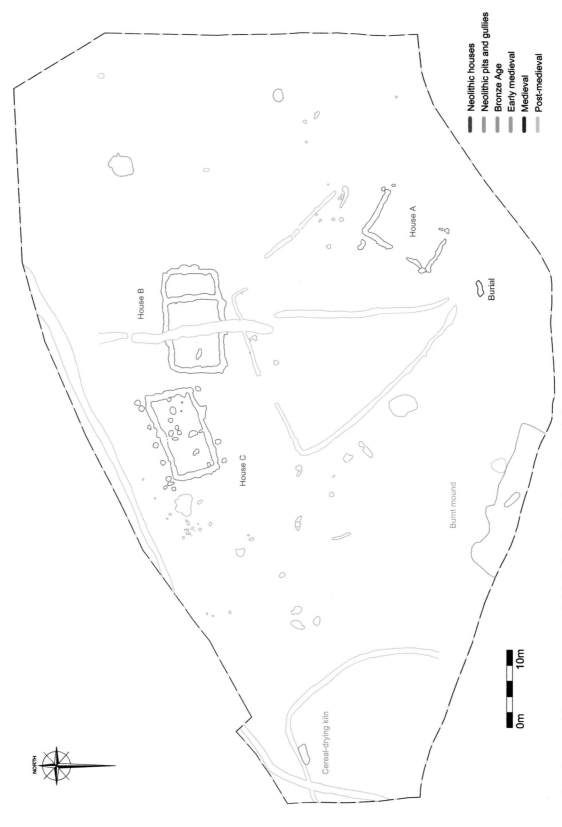

Illus. 2—Plan of excavated features at Monanny (Irish Archaeological Consultancy Ltd)

NORTH

Neolithic houses
Neolithic pits and gullies
Bronze Age
Early medieval
Medieval
Post-medieval

House A
House B
House C
Burial
Burnt mound
Cereal-drying kiln

0m
10m

Illus. 3—Aerial view of Monanny, looking south-west (Studio Lab)

The first farmers in County Monaghan

There is evidence throughout County Monaghan of the religious/social centres of the Neolithic population in the form of megalithic tombs. Monanny has provided the first evidence of where the Neolithic people in this part of the country actually settled and set up home. These Neolithic people were Ireland's first farmers. The settlers would have cleared the forest at this meander of the Longfield River, built their homes from the plentiful supply of wood and farmed the land along the river's edge, growing wheat and barley and possibly raising cattle, pig and sheep. It is possible that fish played a part in their diet, as the adjacent river would have provided a plentiful supply, especially in late summer/autumn.

The focus of Neolithic activity at Monanny was centred on three rectangular buildings, interpreted here as houses (Houses A, B and C; Illus. 4). These have been interpreted as houses on the basis of the large quantity of occupation debris (broken pottery, cooking waste) associated with them and the fact that Houses B and C had well-defined internal hearths. These houses would have been constructed using posts and planks, with perhaps thatch or timber roofing. All of the houses returned radiocarbon dates of c. 4000 BC (see Appendix 1 for details).

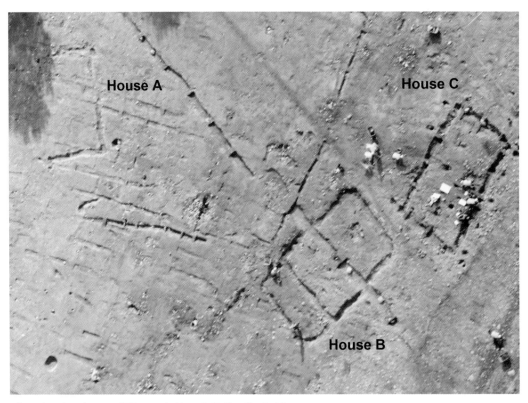

Illus. 4—Aerial view of Houses A, B and C (Studio Lab)

House A

House A was the smallest of the three houses and was situated close to the edge of the river to the south of the site. It was defined by a shallow, subrectangular foundation trench measuring c. 10 m north-east–south-west by 6–7 m. The internal floor area was 54 m². No trace of the southern wall survived, and a possible entrance threshold was identified in the north-west corner. A number of stone-packed post-holes were associated with the southern limits of the eastern and western walls, with some evidence of support posts cut into the packing material. It was clear that the main load-bearing posts were at the four corners of the building, while the foundation trench would have supported upright planks. No internal features were present.

Excavation revealed that the house walls were mostly based on a bed of redeposited natural subsoil, which was evident along the length of the foundation trench. Planks and posts would have been placed on this, with packing material placed around the structural elements. The position of posts was revealed by circular voids in this packing material. These voids were created by the removal of the structural posts and planks and were eventually filled by occupation debris after the probable deliberate abandonment of the house. This debris consisted of charcoal-rich clays with abundant amounts of Early Neolithic pottery.

The western wall of House A seemed to have been burnt down, which probably led to the abandonment of the house, as there was no evidence of rebuilding. This was revealed by a distinct level of burning and an *in situ* burnt timber in the foundation trench. The burnt timber has been identified as oak, which is a common building material for Neolithic houses in Ireland. It is likely that this wood type was chosen as the main construction material for all three houses. The burning of the west wall was probably accidental fire damage rather than the deliberate destruction of the house.

House B

House B was the largest house at Monanny. It was rectangular and measured c. 13.5 m east–west by 8 m externally. The internal floor area was 78 m². The foundation trench varied in depth from 0.2 m to 0.3 m and was generally U-shaped in profile. The house was divided internally by a partition wall forming two rooms (Rooms 1 & 2).

House B was of post-and-plank construction. It appeared to have been deliberately abandoned in the final stages of its life, as evidenced by the complete removal of the posts and planks. The process of removing the structural elements disturbed much of the packing fills in the foundation trench. However, evidence of the location of the posts and planks survived as voids in distinct packing or base material throughout most of the foundation trench. The largest post-holes were central to the north and south walls of the house and may have been the main roof supports (there were no significant internal or external structural features). Substantial post-holes were also evident at the corners and at the junction between the inner, dividing wall and the north and south walls. The foundation trench would have supported the plank walls of the house, with subsidiary posts for extra support where necessary. The subsidiary posts were evident in occasional post-holes at the base of the foundation trench. A lower stone-packed deposit was noted throughout most of the foundation trench and would have acted as a firm footing for the posts and planks. The

Illus. 5—Threshold of House B, during excavation (Irish Archaeological Consultancy Ltd)

Illus. 6—Stone axehead from House B (Claire Phelan)

stone-packed deposit varied in form from thin lenses of small stone to large clusters of rough stone packing.

A burnt timber (oak) was uncovered within the southern wall of the building. This may be the result of limited fire damage during the lifespan of the house, as this is the only point where evidence of burning is present. This part of the wall was probably replaced or mended, as this burnt timber was embedded in the lower levels of the foundation trench and evidently belonged to an early phase of the life of the house.

The entrance to the house was defined by an impressive stone-based threshold in the north-west corner (Illus. 5). This consisted of a series of closely packed flat stones. A post-hole adjacent to, and west of, the threshold may have acted as a door jamb.

Access to the larger of the two rooms (Room 1) defined by the internal wall division would have been via the entrance. A hearth central to the western end of the room was defined by a distinct area of burning. This room would possibly have acted as the main living area. The smaller room (Room 2) may have acted as a storage space for grain or other supplies or as an animal stall when needed. An entrance to this room was tentatively identified at the north-west corner, where the foundation trench was significantly shallower. It is possible, however, that the internal wall was removed during the lifespan of the house to create one large living area. The archaeological evidence pointed to the complete removal of this wall (perhaps it was dug out), with the trench quickly backfilled with occupational debris. This debris produced large quantities of broken pottery sherds, lithics and plant remains.

A polished stone axehead was also recovered from House B (Illus. 6). It was made from porphyritic dolerite. Interestingly, the axehead appeared to have been ground down from a larger/earlier axehead. The axehead was smashed, perhaps deliberately, by repeated blows to its cutting edge (B Leon, pers. comm.) and was deposited in an upright position (blade down) in the packing material of a post support, at the junction of the south wall and the internal wall. It may have been placed there as part of a ritual process during the construction of the house.

House C

House C was the most impressive of the three houses (Illus. 7), as it was sturdier and more architecturally impressive than Houses A and B. The north and south walls would have been flanked by large posts on the exterior of the building, and internal posts would have helped to support the roof. It measured c. 12 m east–west by 7 m (8.5 m including the external

Illus. 7—House C during excavation, looking south-west (Irish Archaeological Consultancy Ltd)

*Illus. 8—Burnt post (*in situ*) in south wall of House C (Irish Archaeological Consultancy Ltd)*

post-holes). The internal floor area was 52 m². The foundation trench was 0.16–0.37 m deep and, in general, had an irregular profile throughout.

There was extensive burning throughout the house. The structural elements (posts and planks) were almost completely burnt or charred through to the base of the foundation trench (Illus. 8). Because House C was burnt *in situ* it offers unusually good evidence of the construction methods of the Neolithic builders. The posts and planks, which have been identified as oak, were held in place in the foundation trench by deposits of packing material incorporating large stones, which were in plentiful supply around the site. The stones were primarily packed on the outer edge of the upright timbers, and presumably this was intended to counteract the outward thrust of the roof weight on the walls. Large posts were situated at the corners, with the walls constructed of planks and occasional supporting (subsidiary) posts. The subsidiary post-holes were spaced evenly throughout the foundation trench at intervals of approximately 0.5–0.75 m.

House C had seven deep post-holes outside the foundation trench on its northern side (Illus. 9). The post-holes were 'doubled up' at the north-west and north-east corners of the building. The main post-holes (c. 0.5 m deep) were 0.2–0.5 m from the outer edge of the trench and were quite evenly spaced, 1.5–1.7 m apart. Three or four of these post-holes tapered to points at the base, suggesting that the posts had been sharpened and driven into the ground. Three post-holes with limited evidence of burning were evident along the outer edge of the southern wall of the building, also set 0.2–0.5 m from the wall. Two were at the southern corners.

Illus. 9—External post-holes of House C, during excavation (Irish Archaeological Consultancy Ltd)

As these post-holes were quite substantial in relation to the foundation trench (in particular the northern post-holes), it is possible that they supplemented the load-bearing post-holes within the corners of the foundation trench. In addition to this they may have carried much of the roof weight or an overhanging eave.

The entrance threshold was identified at the southern end of the eastern wall. The foundation trench was distinctly narrower and shallower at this point, and there was no evidence of burning. Two post-holes immediately inside the house at this point may have been part of a doorframe or small entrance lobby about 2 m wide.

Unlike Houses A and B, there was clear evidence of internal supports in this building. A number of fairly evenly spaced post-holes were uncovered. A well-defined hearth was also identified central to, and close to, the north wall on what may have been the original floor surface of the house.

A possible 'working area' was identified immediately north-west of House C. This area consisted of a number of small patches of burning and a quantity of stake-holes and pits. The main area of burning was central to a cluster of stake-holes, which may have defined the supports for a spit over a fire. In addition to this, a small number of isolated, scattered pits were uncovered throughout the site.

One of the most striking aspects of House C was the evidence of extensive burning. The extent of the burning of the structural elements was so great that it is tempting to view this as evidence of a deliberate act of destruction by fire. This phenomenon has been identified on numerous sites in central and eastern Europe (Stevanovic 1997). The near-complete burning of House C at Monanny could not have resulted accidentally. Experiments have shown that a wooden structure cannot be completely burnt without the use of additional fuel and good draught (Gordon 1953; Bankoff & Winter 1979). It is probable, therefore, that the burning of House C was a deliberate act. Complete burning would require control and purpose, perhaps as part of a ritual act. It has been suggested that the ritual burning of a house could have been carried out in response to the death of a leading member of the family, or simply in response to the end of its usefulness (Cooney 2000). In this latter scenario the house also has 'died'. Bailey (1996, 148) suggests that a house must be treated as having multiple functions and meanings. He states that houses have biographies: that they are conceived, born, live and die, are inhumed or cremated, and are remembered after death.

Artefacts

Large quantities of Early Neolithic pottery sherds were recovered from the three houses. The pottery was mostly retrieved from charcoal-rich occupation deposits. In some cases these deposits had made their way into the foundation trenches after the removal of the structural timbers, but they were also found within the primary construction (packing) material. In addition, large quantities were recovered from the burnt horizons of House C. The pottery assemblage is highly significant and consisted of 978 sherds of Neolithic pottery, representing at least 82 and probably more than 143 vessels. These include plain carinated bowls, uncarinated vessels, a short–necked pot and small cups. Outside of the complex of Lough Gur, Co. Limerick, and the prolific Neolithic sites of north-east Ulster, this is the largest assemblage of plain carinated bowls in Ireland (E Grogan & H Roche, pers. comm.).

A total of 47 flint artefacts was recovered, mostly consisting of flakes, a small number of unworked pieces, a quantity of modified tools and debitage (waste fragments) resulting from the process of tool production. A leaf-shaped arrowhead, a scraper and some form of cutting tool were recovered from House B, and a fine knife was recovered from House C. Half of the modified flint assemblage from Monanny was burnt, most of which was recovered from House B. There was a distinct lack of flint cores (the primary material from which flint tools are made), which is particularly unusual in Early Neolithic flint assemblages (E Nelis, pers. comm.). It is possible that at Monanny only the finer/final stages of flint tool production took place on-site and that the primary flint working took place elsewhere. This is in contrast to most Irish Early Neolithic house sites, where the material seems to have arrived in its raw state to be worked into cores and then later reduced to create tools. Overall, the flint assemblage was small, certainly in comparison to the large quantity of pottery found on the site. This was probably because the people living at Monanny had limited access to flint.

In addition to the flint artefacts, there were artefacts consisting of mudstone and shale cutting tools. In the Irish Neolithic, stone tools were predominantly made from flint; however, other, readily available stone materials were used on sites where the flint resource was limited, as at Monanny. In addition to the cutting tools, hammer/rubbing stones/pounders were found. A serpentine (stone) bead was also found in the burnt horizon of House C.

Environmental evidence

The houses at Monanny were mostly constructed of oak. Oak has great strength and durability and was commonly used for structural timbers during the Neolithic. The oak probably grew in mixed woodlands adjacent to Monanny.

A small quantity of plant remains, hazelnut shells and unidentifiable burnt mammal bone was recovered from the soils sampled from the site. Emmer wheat (*Triticum dicoccum*) was recovered from Houses A and B. Naked barley (*Hordeum vulgare* var. *nudum)* was recovered from House C. Both grain types have been recorded from various Neolithic occupation sites throughout Ireland (Monk 1986).

Dating

On the basis of the radiocarbon dates for the three houses (see Appendix 1) it is entirely possible that Houses A, B and C were contemporary with each other. However, although the pottery from Houses A and C was very similar, there was a higher percentage of more extravagant shoulder pottery sherds from House B. This suggests a slightly later date for this house, or, alternatively, it may simply indicate a more subtle preference in a contemporaneous community (E Grogan & H Roche, pers. comm.).

The dates for the houses at Monanny were obtained from oak charcoal. It is intended to obtain further dates from burnt mammal bone and carbonised seeds to supplement these, as the oak dates may be subject to the 'old wood effect' (i.e. the age of the wood sample may be greater than the age of the archaeological layer or building in which it was found).

Conclusion

The bypass of Carrickmacross provided a unique transect through time in this area. The site at Monanny adds significantly to our knowledge of Neolithic habitation sites in Ireland and is a major archaeological find for County Monaghan. There is every reason to expect that more Neolithic habitation sites like this lie hidden under the rich, rolling agricultural lands around Monanny.

Acknowledgements

First and foremost, the writer thanks the excellent archaeological excavation team. Thanks to Dr Eoin Grogan and Helen Roche for the pottery identifications, help and observations. Thanks to Dr Eiméar Nelis for the lithic analysis, Susan Lyons (Headland Archaeology Ltd) for the plant remains analysis and Ellen OCarroll for charcoal and wood identifications, and also to Barbara Leon (Stone Axe Project), Dr Alison Sheridan, Prof. Gabriel Cooney, Cathy Gibbons and Jessica Smyth. Thanks also to Claire Phelan for her work on the illustrations and to all the staff at Irish Archaeological Consultancy Ltd. The project archaeologist on the N2 Carrickmacross Bypass was Niall Roycroft, Meath County Council National Roads Design Office.

3. Excavation of an early medieval vertical watermill at Killoteran, County Waterford

Donald Murphy and Stuart Rathbone

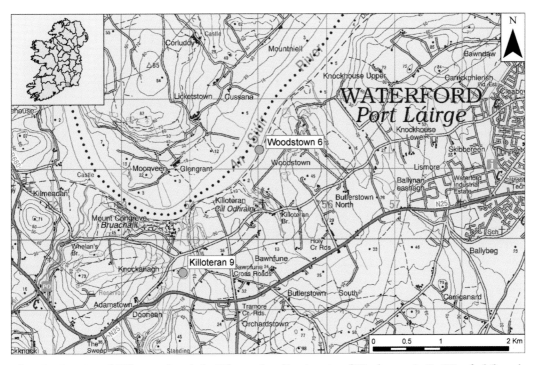

Illus. 1—Location of Killoteran 9 and the Hiberno-Scandinavian site of Woodstown 6, Co. Waterford (based on the Ordnance Survey Ireland map)

During archaeological testing along the route of the N25 Waterford City Bypass in December 2003, structural timbers were exposed in Dooneen Marsh in the townland of Killoteran, Co. Waterford (Illus. 1). Dooneen Marsh is at the base of a small valley leading toward the River Suir to the north (Illus. 2). It is a very poorly drained area, with a small stream running through the centre and a second stream flowing around the eastern side. In modern times attempts have been made to drain the marsh, but the area is still very wet and prone to flooding. Radiocarbon dates from an oak plank and a yew post suggested that the wooden structure had been built in the late Iron Age or at the beginning of the early medieval period (see below), and it was decided to carry out a full excavation in order to reveal the extent and nature of the structure, now designated as archaeological site Killoteran 9 (NGR 253900, 109530; height 0 m OD; excavation licence no. 03E0406).

Excavation on behalf of the National Roads Authority, Waterford County Council, Waterford City Council and Kilkenny County Council was undertaken by Archaeological Consultancy Services Ltd from June to October 2004. The site was found to consist of the well-preserved remains of a substantial, vertical watermill. The excavation was continually hampered by the regular inundation of the site by water seeping out of the surrounding marsh and it was halted in October 2004 owing to a severe flooding event that left the

Illus. 2—Killoteran 9 in Dooneen Marsh, from the south (Studio Lab)

entire marsh under 0.5 m of water. The site was allowed to remain flooded in order to protect the exposed remains, and the level of water has been monitored since then. Some minor work was carried out in October 2005, but, with conditions worsening, it was decided to abandon the site again. Work is due to recommence in the spring and summer of 2006 when conditions become workable once more.

The mill at Killoteran

The mill was fed by a well-constructed mill-race that had an average width of 3 m. The mill-race diverted part of the flow of a small stream that ran to the west of the mill, and a tail-race immediately north of the mill-house emptied the water back into the stream a short distance downstream. Immediately to the south-west of the mill the race widened into a small, semicircular millpond, with a maximum width of 7 m (Illus. 3). The sides of the pond were lined with layers of brushwood, including some very substantial branches. The branches had been laid at right angles to the edge of the pond, running with the slope, and some had been secured in place with substantial stakes.

The flow of water to the mill-wheel was controlled by two wooden dams, both 5 m long and spaced 3.5 m apart (Illus. 4). The dams were constructed of oak planks set longitudinally into a slotted oak base plate. The base plate was set into alluvium on the bed of the mill-race and was cut into the sides of the channel and held in place by two large posts, one at either end. The gaps between the planks were filled with moss and alluvial clay in order to waterproof the dam. The bed of the channel downstream of the first dam was considerably lower than the bed of the millpond above the first dam, and it is assumed that the full original height of the second dam would therefore have been lower than the height of the first dam. If this was the case, the water level between the dams would have been correspondingly lower than the water level in the millpond. This is consistent with the surviving heights of the posts that were used to secure the sides of the dams, but, of course, the surviving heights do not necessarily correspond to their original heights.

The flow of water across the dams would have been controlled by sluice gates or openings at the centre of each dam. The two dams were clearly contemporary with each other and would have worked in unison. The upstream dam probably had a sluice gate near its top, but no evidence of this survived. This dam was used to retain water in the millpond and maintain a constant level of water in the reservoir between the two dams. A small, rectangular opening found in the centre of the second dam, near to its base, represented the remains of a sluice opening (Illus. 5). Only the lower part of this opening was recovered, as the dam did not survive much above this point, and, therefore, its overall size and the amount of water it would have allowed through can only be estimated. The width of the opening was approximately 0.3 m. This was used to regulate the flow of water past the waterwheel; being so low down, it would have let water through under pressure. If the reservoir between the two dams was maintained at a constant level by manipulating a sluice gate on the first dam, water coming through the opening at the bottom of the second dam would always flow at the same speed and volume. If this interpretation is correct, then the people who constructed the mill used sophisticated engineering techniques to deliver very precise control over the volume and speed of water flowing past the waterwheel.

A final point is worth noting with regard to the management of the flow of water into the mill: the excavations that have taken place so far have identified traces of a possible overflow channel, which ran from the north-eastern end of the millpond around the east of the mill itself to join up directly with the tail-race (Illus. 6). One of the first priorities upon resuming work at the site will be to verify the existence of this feature.

The main workings of the mill were constructed immediately beyond the lower dam, on the north-west side of the channel. The workings consisted of the wheel-pit and the mill-house. The wheel-pit was in a position central to the dams and in line with the mill-race. It consisted of a rectangular area, 2 m long and 1.5 m wide. The pit could have held a wheel with an estimated diameter of up to 1.8 m, but it seems more likely that it held a smaller wheel with a fast rate of spin rather than a large wheel turning more slowly. A small, rapidly rotating wheel is known in modern terms as a flutter wheel, and this design would be consistent with the small size of the opening in the second dam. The wheel-pit was lined on both sides with a series of planks lying sideways on top of each other and held in place by wooden posts at either end. These plank walls would have retained the earth-cut channel on either side of the wheel. The floor of the wheel-pit was lined with large planks that would have prevented the flowing water from scouring out the bottom of the channel and thereby reducing the efficiency of the wheel. The axle of the wheel would have been supported on both sides of the channel and would have exerted pressure on the permanently sodden ground to either side. While the structure of the mill-house would have retained this force on the north-west side of the channel, it was the plank-built revetment of the side of the channel that performed this task to the south-east. Additional support on the south-eastern side was provided by the lower dam and by a second revetment aligned at right angles to the channel and running away from the north-east corner of the wheel-pit.

N

Tail-race

Mill-house

Wheel-pit

Possible Sluice

Reservoir

Fence

Possible Sluice

Lower Dam

Upper Dam

Millpond

Mill-race

5 metres

Illus. 3—Plan of main structural features (Archaeological Consultancy Services Ltd)

Illus. 4—Photograph showing main elements of the mill's design (Archaeological Consultancy Services Ltd)

Illus. 5—Photograph of wheel-pit under excavation, showing rectangular opening in lower dam (Archaeological Consultancy Services Ltd)

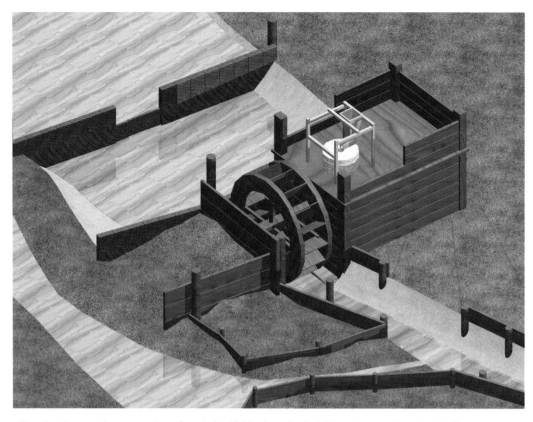

Illus. 6—Suggested reconstruction of vertical mill (Archaeological Consultancy Services Ltd)

The mill-house was situated along the north-west side of the wheel, where portions of two upright plank-lined walls were exposed. The first of these walls was formed by the north-west end of the lower dam, and the second was formed by planks laid on their edge and held by two large posts at a distance of 2 m from the first wall. The floor of the mill-house was constructed from a mixture of imported clay and turf. The overall dimensions were small, approximately 3 m by 2 m. Despite its small area, the mill-house may have been quite a tall structure, as it had to contain the axle of the waterwheel, a set of gears, a vertical drive shaft, a set of millstones and any hoppers that may have been used.

Beyond the main workings of the mill, a small tail-race was exposed, consisting of a small channel, only 2 m wide, cut into the alluvium. This was revetted on both sides with reused timbers secured by small posts. The remains of a small wattle fence were exposed along the south-east side of the tail-race, and this may have been used to stop surface water from flowing in and causing a backwash onto the wheel.

More than 600 fragments of wood were recovered, in addition to the mill structure itself. For the most part, these consisted of unworked branches that either had been washed along the mill-race or were used to revet the edges of the millpond. Worked fragments were also recovered, including planks, posts, a possible wheel-shaft and possible mill-wheel paddles.

Artefacts

A total of 21 upper and lower millstone fragments were recovered from the tail-race in the vicinity of the mill-house. These stones were all made from locally quarried Old Grey Sandstone. Millstones would have broken on a regular basis and would have been discarded nearby. The original diameter of one of the millstones has been calculated from the curvature of one fragment. The diameter was estimated to have been 0.53 m, which would have made the stone reasonably small and light and supports the interpretation that the waterwheel itself had a small diameter and a fast rotation.

A small number of other artefacts were recovered from this site; as would be expected with a waterlogged site, many of them were made from organic materials. Organic finds included six pieces of worked antler, a bone knife-handle, two fragments of leather and a 0.5 m length of rope. Non-organic finds included iron nails and rivets, a bronze chain link, five whetstones, two small pieces of slag and a circular slate fragment with a central perforation. A small amount of animal bone was also recovered and included cattle remains and antler. Detailed analysis of these finds is under way, but preliminary work indicates that they are early medieval in date. A possible hammerstone and a flint flake of prehistoric date were also recovered from the fill of the mill-race, but these may be residual objects unrelated to the mill.

Site abandonment

Although excavation of this site is incomplete and further work may reveal additional features, it is thought that the structure represents a single building phase, with the possibility of some running repairs and slight modifications to the design. The site may have been abandoned because, despite the builders' efforts to control water-flow through the mill, the area was too prone to flooding to be viable. (This speculation is based on our own experience of the rapid way in which water inundates this area.) Once the mill was abandoned, it rapidly silted up, and it was this silting that protected so much of the superstructure and ensured its survival. The mill was exposed below 2 m of alluvium, indicating quite considerable silting since the site was abandoned.

The mill-race was itself cut into alluvium that had accumulated here before construction of the mill. The massive accumulation of this alluvium was probably due to a number of factors in the surrounding landscape. The first of these was the fact that the site floods during high tides on the River Suir. Secondly, the area is in a basin between the hills of Killoteran and Adamstown. A number of prehistoric habitation sites were found on the hill at Adamstown, dating to the first and second millenniums BC, and, more recently, evidence of habitation during the same period was discovered on the hill in Killoteran. The presence of these sites would suggest that farming was being carried out in the immediate locality since at least the Early Bronze Age, and perhaps tillage had the effect of emptying silt into the basin below. This process is likely to have continued until early medieval times, and the accumulation of silt may have increased the frequency of flooding episodes and infilling of the mill structure. The abandonment of the mill may also have come about as a result of climate change, which led to almost continual flooding of the area. It is worth noting that, although considerable effort has gone into draining this area in recent times— both through the canalisation of the original stream so that it now runs to the east of the mill and through the use of a very extensive network of field drains—this area still floods regularly and spends much of the winter covered in water.

The stream that the mill-race was linked to flowed into the River Suir, which is some 800 m north of the mill. Interestingly, the Suir is currently tidal to a point a short distance upstream from the confluence with this stream, and at high tide this stream may well have backed up with tidal floodwater. However, it would be a mistake to consider this site to be a tidal mill, as these are typically situated on shorelines. There is no evidence that the structure was adapted to take advantage of this tidal backflow, and the stream itself would have been sufficient to maintain the height of water in the millpond. Indeed, if the area was inundated with water during high tide, it would have been an inconvenience to the operators of the mill; as such flooding would have temporarily stopped their operations.

Dating

As mentioned above, two radiocarbon dates were obtained from a yew post and an oak plank exposed during the preliminary phase of this project. The samples returned dates of AD 340–600 and AD 410–650 (see Appendix 1 for details), which, taken at face value, are significantly earlier than most other dates so far obtained from other Irish watermills, of either horizontal or vertical type. Forty-two mills have been excavated and dated in Ireland. The dates range from the mid-first millennium AD to the 14th century, with a significant concentration from the early eighth century to the early 10th century (Brady, in press). It is unfortunate that the dates so far obtained from Killoteran 9 have such large deviations, ranging as they do from the fourth to the seventh century, but it is hoped that the structure will be precisely dated in the future using dendrochronology (tree-ring dating). It will be particularly interesting to see whether the Killoteran 9 site fits neatly alongside other early seventh-century examples, such as Nendrum, Co. Down, and Little Island, Co. Cork, or the site extends the known use of watermills in Ireland back into the fifth or even the fourth century.

Ecclesiastical association?

With regard to the location of the mill, it is probably significant that the boundary of Killoteran townland juts out into the marsh in an unusual manner at this point (Illus. 7). This deviation from the general north–south alignment of the boundary may be related specifically to the mill's location and may represent a desire to incorporate it into Killoteran townland. It is tempting to infer that the mill may, therefore, have been associated with the early ecclesiastical establishment of St Otteran, situated less than a mile to the north-east in the same townland. Little is known about St Otteran's itself, but it was probably the centre of an ecclesiastical estate. Killoteran church is described as being in ruins in an ecclesiastical survey of 1615, but the site probably dates back to the sixth century. A holy well is situated 300 m WNW of the church. The name Killoteran is translated as Cill Odhrain, or 'Church of St Odran', a sixth-century saint who later became a patron saint of the Vikings and was chosen as patron saint of the city of Waterford in 1096. Recent research into such establishments has suggested that their economic clout and ability to organise and manage

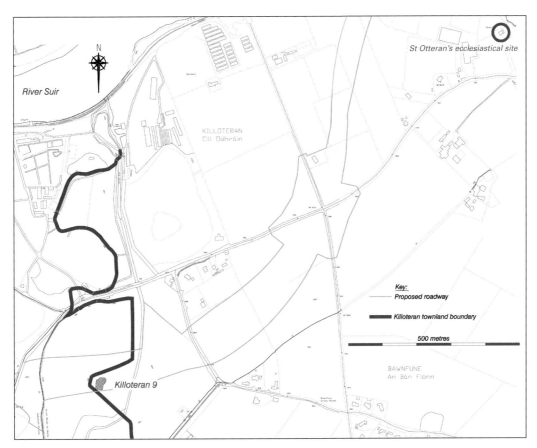

Illus. 7—Map showing location of Killoteran 9 and townland boundary extending into the marsh to include the mill (Archaeological Consultancy Services Ltd, based on the Ordnance Survey Ireland map)

landscapes have previously been underestimated (Doherty 2000). St Otteran's is the most likely candidate to be the patron of this sophisticated mill, and its connection to the early levels of occupation at the Hiberno-Scandinavian site of Woodstown 6—elsewhere on the River Suir (Illus. 1)—also requires examination (O'Brien & Russell 2005, 118–20). Two more unusual and unexplained kinks in the townland boundary occur between the site of the mill at Killoteran and the River Suir, and investigations in these areas might reveal traces of subsequent mills built to replace Killoteran 9 once it had become unusable, although this is highly speculative.

Conclusion

The mill at Killoteran has great potential to develop the study of milling technology in early Ireland. Future work will focus on dating the construction of the site more accurately, examining the lower portions of the superstructure and looking for evidence of earlier activity at the site. Once excavation is complete, it should be possible to model the flow of water through the mill accurately and to calculate how much energy the mill would have generated. Excavations in Ireland have already made significant contributions to the understanding of the development of milling technology in Europe. The excavation of Killoteran 9 has great potential to add to our understanding of this process.

Acknowledgements

Thanks to Richard O'Brien, project archaeologist, Tramore House Regional Design Office, and to Ian Russell (excavation director) and Gillian McCarthy (supervisor) for their work on the excavation. Thanks also to Aidan Kenny, Martin Halpin and Niall Gillespie for the illustrations. Thanks to Dr Colin Rynne, University College Cork, for his help and advice regarding the excavation, and to William E Hogg, President of the Mills and Millers of Ireland, for his site visit and interest in the project.

4. Archaeological discoveries on a new section of the N2 in Counties Meath and Dublin

Maria FitzGerald

Archaeological investigations in advance of the N2 Finglas–Ashbourne road scheme revealed approximately 20 new archaeological sites interspersed along the route (Illus. 1). Their date range indicates that there was intermittent human activity in the Finglas–Ashbourne area during at least the past 5,000 years. The diverse nature of this activity is reflected by a range of site types, including short-term dispersed occupation pits and features, burnt mound sites, small-scale kiln and industrial sites, and extensive habitation complexes, as well as sites of ritual, burial or ceremonial significance.

The N2 road scheme comprises c. 17 km of dual carriageway extending NNE from the existing N2/M50 junction in Dublin, bypassing the busy and congested town of Ashbourne, Co. Meath, on its western side before rejoining the existing N2 north of the town. The archaeological works for the scheme were carried out on behalf of the National Roads Authority and Meath County Council.

All the sites discussed here were fully excavated during 2004 and 2005 by Cultural Resource Development Services Ltd (CRDS Ltd). Preliminary archaeological investigations for the scheme commenced in 2001, however, with a contribution on archaeology to the Environmental Impact Statement prepared by Valerie J Keeley Ltd. Subsequently, an aerial survey of the route was carried out by Margaret Gowen & Co. Ltd in 2001, and an extensive geophysical survey of the route was carried out by GSB Prospection Ltd in 2002. Cumulatively, these investigations identified a number of existing and new archaeological sites along and adjacent to the route. In order to investigate their potential, and that of the entire route, an extensive programme of test excavations was carried out between August and November 2003 by Judith Carroll Network Archaeology Ltd.

Summary of archaeological discoveries

Given the breadth of evidence revealed and the limited length of this paper, it is proposed to present a preliminary overview of the findings and subsequently to discuss some of the more interesting sites and artefacts in greater detail.

Prehistoric sites
Most of the new sites revealed were prehistoric in date, or at least had a primary phase of activity during the prehistoric period. With the exception of two burial ring-ditches at Coldwinters, Co. Dublin (Record of Monuments and Places [RMP] No. ME014-015), and Killegland, Co. Meath (ME045-002), comparatively little prehistoric activity had been recorded in the vicinity of the route in advance of the N2 investigations. The earliest site discovered along the route was Site 5, a Neolithic (3200–2800 BC) henge or ritual enclosure at Kilshane, Co. Dublin. Excavation revealed an intriguing ritual and burial site, and a summary of the findings is presented below.

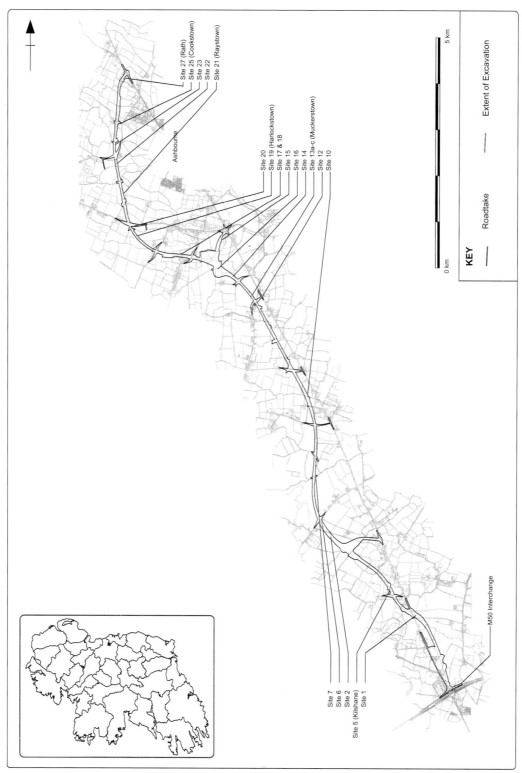

Illus. 1—Location of N2 Finglas–Ashbourne road scheme, Counties Meath and Dublin (CRDS Ltd, based on Ordnance Survey Ireland map)

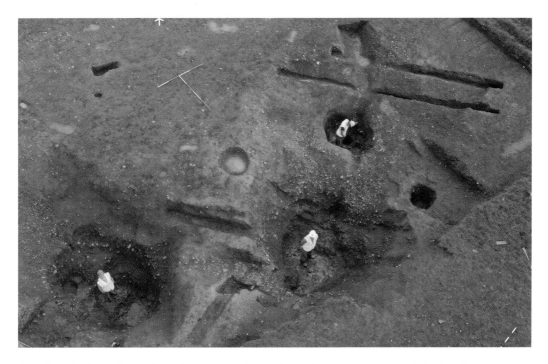

Illus. 2—Overhead view of deep pits or wells at Site 13b, Muckerstown, Co. Meath (Hawkeye)

Many of the other prehistoric sites were of Bronze Age date. These included some very large, deep, waterlogged pits or wells of Middle Bronze Age date (Illus. 2) discovered at Muckerstown (Site 13b), Co. Meath. The pits produced an assemblage of unique wooden artefacts that are discussed in greater detail below.

The most ubiquitous prehistoric site type in Ireland is the burnt mound, and five sites of this type were found interspersed along the route in the townlands of Coldwinters (Site 1), Co. Dublin, Ward Lower (Site 7), Co. Dublin, Harlockstown (two sites—Sites 20 and 31), Co. Meath, and Baltrasna (Site 15), Co. Meath. Burnt mounds are largely dated to the Bronze Age, though some earlier and later examples are recorded. They are generally interpreted as cooking sites, but alternative processes that use quantities of hot water—such as saunas, leather preparation, cloth-fulling and cloth-dyeing—have also been proposed.

Other prehistoric sites along the scheme included a small isolated pit at Ward Upper (Site 6), Co. Dublin, which produced c. 600 sherds (representing 24 vessels) of Late Bronze Age pottery (c. 1150–800 BC). The pit may simply have been used for refuse, but given the extent of the pottery assemblage it could also be interpreted as reflecting a more complex ritual deposition in the landscape. Extensive Bronze Age and Iron Age burial and habitation complexes were discovered at Harlockstown (Site 19) and Rath (Site 27), Co. Meath, and these sites are also discussed in more detail below.

Early medieval sites
Prior to the N2 investigations, early medieval activity in the Finglas/Ashbourne landscape was represented by ringforts, souterrains and early church sites extensively listed in the RMP (ringforts at Wotton (ME045-022) and Muckerstown (ME045-021), a cropmark enclosure at Killegland (ME045-003), a souterrain at Baltrasna (ME045-026), and early

Illus. 3—Segment of ringfort ditch at Cookstown, Co. Meath—an early medieval farmstead enclosure partly underlying a modern farmstead (Hawkeye)

church sites at Donaghmore (ME045-008), Killegland (ME045-004) and Cookstown (ME045-001)). New archaeological sites revealed by the N2 investigations add considerably to this evidence. At the southern end of the scheme, a small, multi-phase cereal-drying kiln and metalworking site (Site 2) was found on a slight rise in the townland of Cherryhound, Co. Dublin. This industrial site had three main phases of activity—a phase of metalworking to the east, followed by phases of kiln activity at the western end of the site. Associated houses and settlements were not discovered but may have been located nearby beyond the road corridor.

At Cookstown, Co. Meath, at the northern end of the scheme, the geophysical survey revealed a circular enclosure (Site 25) located partly within the roadtake but extending under an inhabited farm to the west of the road. Excavation confirmed that this enclosure was an early medieval ringfort (Illus. 3). A ring-pin and the ring portion of a second pin were recovered from primary ditch fills.

The most extensive and significant early medieval settlement complex was uncovered at Raystown (Site 21), Co. Meath. This was a greenfield site before the N2 investigations and was first identified during the geophysical survey of 2002. The initial survey was subsequently extended to areas outside the roadtake in order to define the full extent and nature of the archaeological features. Approximately one third of the site was within the area affected by the road scheme and this area was fully excavated during 2004 by CRDS Ltd. The excavation director, Matthew Seaver, discusses the results of the Raystown excavation more extensively elsewhere in this volume.

Medieval and post-medieval sites

The medieval period is well represented, particularly at the southern end of the road scheme, by upstanding monuments such as Dunsoghly Castle (DU014-00501), Co. Dublin, and Hiberno-Norman mottes at Donaghmore (ME045-007), Co. Meath, and Kilshane (DU014-001) and Newtown (DU014-013), Co. Dublin. Newly discovered medieval sites recorded along the scheme at Cookstown (Site 25), Baltrasna (Site 17/18) and Muckerstown (Site 12/13a), Co. Meath, add to this picture of medieval settlement. Cookstown was a multi-period site with an important phase of medieval rural activity and settlement. The sites at Baltrasna and Muckerstown were interpreted as medieval farmsteads. The evidence at Baltrasna represented the remains of a field system and cobbled laneway from the late medieval period. The site at Muckerstown consisted of the yards, kitchen gardens and infields of a medieval and post-medieval settlement. This site produced about 2000 sherds of medieval pottery of predominantly local wares, dating from the 13th/14th centuries. The new evidence from the scheme augments the picture of high-status, defensive mottes and castles by revealing dispersed medieval rural settlements and farms.

Kilshane Henge

The earliest and one of the most significant sites from the scheme was a Neolithic ritual enclosure (Illus. 4), 37 m by 27 m, discovered at the southern end of the scheme at Kilshane, Co. Dublin (NGR 311010, 242951; height 81.3 m OD; excavation licence no. 03E1359 extension; Excavation Director Dermot Moore). The artefactual evidence from pottery and stone tools indicates that this site had its origins in the Middle Neolithic period

Illus. 4—Elevated view of irregular henge enclosure at Kilshane, Co. Dublin (Hawkeye)

Illus. 5—Animal bone layer undergoing excavation at Kilshane Neolithic henge, Co. Dublin (Hawkeye)

(3200–2800 BC), but it also saw intermittent activity during the Late Neolithic and Early and Middle Bronze Age periods. The enclosing ditch was formed by the excavation of a series of intercutting and overlapping ditch segments. With the exception of some 'cleaned-out' cremation pits and a crouched inhumation burial, all thought to have been of Early Bronze Age date, few features were recorded within the interior. A unique element of this site was the recovery of approximately 300 kg of cattle bone from the base of the ditch segments (Illus. 5). Sherds from globular bowls dating from the Middle Neolithic were also discovered in the ditch fills, sealing the animal bone, and these indicate a similar deposition date.

This is the largest assemblage of Neolithic animal bone from Ireland to date. Approximately 40 to 50 immature cattle are represented, and these were deposited in the ditch segments in both a disarticulated and an articulated state. In some instances, certain bone types, such as long bones, were grouped together. According to Dr Finbar McCormick (Queen's University, Belfast) the bone was defleshed, but there is little evidence for bone disease or butchery. The bone must have been covered over very soon after its deposition, as there is little evidence for animal gnawing of the bone. Nearly all of the animals were slaughtered at 18 months old, indicating that the event took place in the autumn. The absence of butchery marks on the disarticulated cattle bone and the presence of articulated animals indicate that the bone assemblage is unlikely to represent the remains of feasting. The evidence would suggest that the animals were slaughtered, disarticulated (in most cases), defleshed and deposited in the ditch segments, and that they represent the remains of animal sacrifice.

The upper fills of the ditch, particularly to the east, contained numerous sherds of pottery and a large assemblage of stone tools. The pottery from this layer included 17 Early Bronze Age Food Vessels (2400–1700 BC), sherds of Vase Urns and Encrusted Urns, as well as twelve Middle Bronze Age Cordoned Urns (2000–1400 BC). Although Food Vessels are occasionally recorded in domestic contexts, it is predominantly a funerary ware. The excavation director, Dermot Moore, suggests that a nearby Early and Middle Bronze Age cemetery may have been cleared out and the contents deposited into the upper fills of the enclosing ditch.

This site appears to be unique, with few obvious Irish parallels. It is comparable to a small group of henges or embanked enclosures, a site type interpreted as being of ritual, ceremonial or burial significance because of the large internal area of the enclosures, the absence of finds from the interiors and the non-defensive nature of the banks. Recorded examples are generally much larger than the Kilshane site, however. The segmented nature of the ditch may also invoke comparisons with the much larger British or European causewayed enclosure sites, interpreted as possible cattle marts or community meeting places. These sites also have limited evidence for internal structural remains but have evidence for the deliberate deposition of pottery, human bone and animal bones in the ditches and in pits. An Early Neolithic causewayed enclosure site was recently discovered at Magheraboy, Co. Sligo (MacDonagh 2005, 17–20), and this site was also interpreted as of ritual significance, with deposits of flint arrowheads, pottery and deliberately broken porcellanite axeheads.

The Kilshane henge may have served as a community meeting place for ceremony and/or burial during the Neolithic and Bronze Age periods. Environmental evidence suggests that the landscape was heavily wooded during this period, so the Kilshane site would have been a large clearing in the forest. Did the local community congregate at Kilshane for an event each autumn or at certain other times? Did each family group walk to the site and bring along an animal that they had herded through the forests and countryside? Was it a dispersed community, and from how far did its members travel? There are no known Neolithic sites in the immediate vicinity, but did people come from nearby Neolithic complexes such as Knowth and Newgrange, 32 km to the north-west, or from houses at Coolfore, Co. Louth (Ó Drisceoil 2002), 26 km to the north-east, and Newtown, Co. Meath, 25 km north-east (Gowen & Halpin 1992)—or from much further afield? The cattle bone could be interpreted as a deliberate symbolic deposition, and there may have been games and sports associated with the killing. Were all the animals killed at or near the site, and could they have been offered up in thanks for a good autumn harvest or in appeasement after a bad one? In addition to ceremonial activities, did the community meet to trade and barter animals and tools, and generally exchange ideas and skills? We can only imagine the festival atmosphere at the site, which was certainly an important local focus for community activity.

Prehistoric Harlockstown

An important prehistoric complex was discovered at Harlockstown (Site 19), Co. Meath. This site (NGR 305304, 250560; height 70.82 m OD; excavation licence no. 03E1526 extension; Excavation Director David O'Connor) was first identified by geophysical survey (Illus. 6), and subsequent excavation revealed a very close correlation between the survey results and the actual site features. Harlockstown was a multi-period and multi-functional site. Primary features comprised an Early Bronze Age circular enclosure (radiocarbon-dated

Illus. 6—Elevated view of prehistoric complex at Harlockstown, Co. Meath, showing Early Bronze Age circular enclosure (left) and square Iron Age enclosure (right) (Studio Lab)

to 1960–1690 BC, Wk-16288; see Appendix 1 for details) cut by a square Iron Age enclosure where extensive metalworking activity took place. Excavation revealed that the circular enclosure was a burial monument with a cremation pit and two inhumations within the interior. There was no evidence for a mound, but the upcast material from the ditch may have been thrown into the enclosure and the burials inserted into the mound material.

The inhumed individuals were placed in a crouched position in stone-lined graves and were accompanied by substantially intact decorated pottery vessels known as Food Vessels (Illus. 7). The vessels have been identified as a ribbed bowl and a necked bipartite bowl with a cruciform motif on the base (E Grogan and H Roche, pers. comm.). Both individuals were adults, one of indeterminate sex but more likely female (radiocarbon-dated to 2120–1870 BC, Wk-16290) and the second possibly male (L Fibiger, pers. comm.). Food Vessel burials are not unusual in Ireland, with dates generally clustering between 2460 BC and 1980 BC. Such inhumations can be found in unmarked or flat cemeteries, or beneath cairns with either burnt or unburnt remains. The pots were originally referred to as Food Vessels because it was assumed that they contained a food offering for the spirit of the deceased. This has yet to be substantiated by any conclusive evidence from residue analysis, however.

Muckerstown wooden artefacts

Two large waterlogged pits or wells, each approximately 2.5 m in depth, were the primary features revealed at Site 13b in Muckerstown, Co. Meath (NGR 307851, 249310; height 70.27 m OD; excavation licence no. 03E1331 extension; Excavation Director Caitríona

Illus. 7—Burial with Food Vessel pot at Harlockstown, Co. Meath (CRDS Ltd)

Moore). One of the pits was lined with a wooden panel, possibly wattlework (radiocarbon-dated to 1390–1080 BC, Wk-16818), and both may have been accessed by sloping sides laid with fine metalled surfaces. Their purpose is uncertain and they may simply have functioned as wells, as they were deep enough for the extraction of groundwater. An alternative processing function—such as basketry, tanning, dyeing or flax preparation, which all use watery pits—is also possible. Both pits produced organic materials, including worked wood, but one of the pits produced a unique assemblage of 130 basketry artefacts.

These artefacts have been analysed by Caitríona Moore and Dr Ingelise Stuijts, who found that they were very deliberately constructed composite artefacts, comprising three elements: a bundle of woody twigs, a thicker central spine and a twisted branch or withy looping around the bundle (Illus. 8). They were primarily made from four species: willow, broom, ash and alder.

One of the artefacts has been radiocarbon-dated to the Middle Bronze Age period (1600–1210 BC, Wk-15499) and, as such, appears to be a unique artefact type with few Irish or European parallels. Their function is uncertain and they compare most closely with a broom called a besom, familiar from folklife evidence in Ireland. It is certainly intriguing that 130 of these objects were discarded or ritually deposited in this pit. The ritual deposition of

Illus. 8—Wooden basketry artefact from Site 13b, Muckerstown, Co. Meath (CRDS Ltd)

artefacts in watery locations is well attested in prehistoric times and the objects may therefore have had a non-functional, symbolic significance (C Moore, pers. comm.).

Prehistoric Rath

An extensive prehistoric complex was discovered at Rath (Site 27), Co. Meath, at the northern end of the scheme, where the new road rejoins the existing N2 (NGR 305049, 254101; height 86 m OD; excavation licence no. 03E1214 extension; Excavation Director Holger Schweitzer). The site complex extended over a large area measuring c. 280 m by 100 m, extending northwards from a stream and rising to a hillcrest with panoramic views. The primary features on site included a possible sweat-lodge adjacent to the stream, three ring-ditches on the highest point of the ridge, a metalworking area, a cereal-drying kiln and some deep, waterlogged pits (to the north of the existing N2). This site produced an extraordinary array of high-status finds, including a female buried wearing toe-rings, an unusual copper-alloy La Tène fibula, segmented faience beads and some prehistoric wooden vessels (radiocarbon-dated to 390–190 BC, Wk-16824).

Sweat-lodge?
Holger Schweitzer, excavation director, interpreted one of the structures as a sweat-lodge. The site was beside the small stream and the building was defined by a circle of large post-holes with a hearth located between two of the post-holes (Illus. 9). The hearth was defined by a double ring of stake-holes and had a flue extending into the interior of the building. The building was surrounded by a curving ditch that may have channelled water from the adjacent stream. The basic principle of such a sweat-lodge or sauna was that stones were heated on a hearth, water poured onto the stones and steam channelled into the lodge via the flue. A trough and a mound of discarded burnt stone were located outside the building.

A disc-headed brooch and fibula were recovered in the vicinity of the building. These dress-fasteners may have been lost during dressing and undressing associated with a sauna.

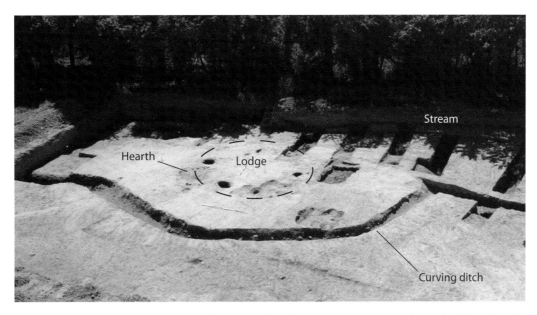

Illus. 9—Sweat-lodge at Rath, Co. Meath: a circle of post-holes within a narrow enclosing ditch (Hawkeye)

The fibula is of late La Tène type and came from the adjacent terrace leading down to the water. Approximately 30 fibulae are known from Ireland. Preliminary examination of this new fibula indicates that the type is unique in Ireland and is paralleled only by British finds (B Raftery, pers. comm.). The introduction of the fibula brooch to Ireland during the Iron Age is thought to reflect changes in clothing such as the wearing of finer wool and linen garments.

Also from this site, recovered from the fill of a small ring-ditch to the north of the building, were three tiny segmented faience beads. Faience is a glass-like substance that is made from simple elements but can be very difficult to produce. The beads from Rath are of an unusual form; they are made from several discs fused together. They appear to be of European morphology but may have been made locally (A Sheridan, pers. comm.). Irish and British faience dates from the Early Bronze Age period (1900–1500 BC). Unusually, however, the Rath beads have come from a context dated to the Iron Age (740–360 BC, Wk-16317). Faience is regarded as a symbol of status but it may also have been worn as a talisman in life and death.

The woman with rings on her toes
One of the most spectacular finds from this site was the burial of a woman in the fills of a small ring-ditch at the north of the site (Illus. 10). The woman was found lying on her side in a crouched position with clasped hands placed under her cheek. On her feet were three copper-alloy toe-rings—two plain spiral rings and a third ring decorated with a herringbone motif. On the right foot, the spiral ring encircled the big toe as well as the tips of the second and possibly the third toe. The decorated toe-ring encircled the fourth toe (Schweitzer 2005, 97, illus. 5). A possible fragment of leather was recorded at her heel. It was not possible to establish the position of the other spiral toe-ring because of the poor preservation of the skeletal remains of the left foot.

Illus. 10—Female burial with toe-rings, Rath, Co. Meath (CRDS Ltd)

The closest parallels for this burial are a small number of high-status Iron Age burials from Britain at sites such as Poundbury Hill (Farwell & Molleson 1993) and Maiden Castle (Wheeler 1943). Most of these burials are male with a toe-ring on one foot, and the rings are interpreted as attachments for leather sandals, which were a sign of sovereignty. However, a burial of a female wearing toe-rings was recently discovered under the floor of a late Iron Age metalworking site at Minehowe, Orkney (Card et al. 2005, 326). Given the paucity of Irish parallels for the woman at Rath, it is tempting to speculate that she was a royal visitor from Britain or at least had very strong cultural connections with that island. The bone has not proved suitable for dating so the burial is dated by comparisons only. Scientists at Bradford University are carrying out isotope analysis on her teeth in order to help build up a picture of her diet, which may yield clues as to her cultural background.

The presence of the fibula and the faience beads indicates that the Rath habitation and burial complex was occupied and used by a high-status wealthy community. Given the exclusively British parallels for the fibula and the burial with toe-rings, it seems possible that this community had strong cultural or trading connections with that island.

Rural medieval settlement at Cookstown

Cookstown (Site 25), Co. Meath, located at the northern end of the scheme, was a multi-period site with an important phase of medieval rural activity (NGR 304938, 253010; height 76.27 m OD; excavation licence no. 03E1252 extension; Excavation Director Richard Clutterbuck). In addition to the aforementioned early medieval ringfort (Illus. 3), the site also had evidence for extensive prehistoric and medieval phases of activity.

Illus. 11—Schematic drawing showing the early medieval ringfort and the row of medieval buildings (Structures I–IV) with infields and kitchen gardens at Cookstown, Co. Meath. Structure I is the building interpreted as a forge (CRDS Ltd)

About 30 m east of the ringfort, a row of medieval structures with infields and kitchen gardens was revealed (Illus. 11). The structures were defined by shallow, enclosing slot-trenches (probably used to hold wooden walls). Richard Clutterbuck, excavation director, has interpreted one of the buildings (Structure 1) as a forge. Central to this structure was a shallow subrectangular trench with silty lower fills, which contained large quantities of iron slag. This may have been used as a quenching trough to cool down the molten metal during manufacture. The central area, which was raised, contained four large post-holes that probably held the base posts of a table. Cookstown produced a large assemblage of metal objects, including knives, a pair of scissors, hooks and nails, and it seems likely that some of these were made on site. In addition to large quantities of slag, some copper was also recovered from the forge, and archaeometallurgical analysis is proposed to assess the types of metalworking that took place here.

The row of buildings fronted onto what is interpreted as a medieval laneway. Few medieval rural buildings or settlements have been excavated to date in Ireland, so the results of the excavation and post-excavation research should greatly enhance our understanding of the nature of medieval rural settlement.

Conclusions

All of the sites discussed above were unknown in advance of the N2 Finglas–Ashbourne road scheme and indicate that human activity in the area was more extensive than previously understood. Additionally, many of these were new site types, not previously recorded or reflected in the RMP for this area, and their discovery has demonstrated that there was greater social diversity and complexity than previously thought. The investigations clearly reveal the potential of future archaeological works to alter our perception and understanding of past societies. It is likely that specialist post-excavation analysis for the N2 project will shed further light on these sites and the activities and ways of life of the people who occupied or visited them. The post-excavation phase of the project is well under way and it is intended to publish the results of the excavations more fully in due course.

Acknowledgements

Thanks to all those involved in the N2 Finglas–Ashbourne road scheme and, in particular, at CRDS Ltd, Senior Archaeologist Finola O'Carroll, Post-excavation Manager Madeleine Murray and Excavation Directors Richard Clutterbuck (Sites 24/25 and 26), Donal Fallon (Sites 12/13a, 13c and 17/18), Caitríona Moore (Sites 16 and 13b), Dermot Moore (Site 5), Cara Murray (Sites 14, 15, 20 and 31), Laurence McGowan (Sites 2, 6 and 22/23), David O'Connor (Site 19), Matthew Seaver (Site 21) and Holger Schweitzer (Sites 1, 7 and 27).

5. Excavation of a ringfort at Leggetsrath West, County Kilkenny

Anne-Marie Lennon

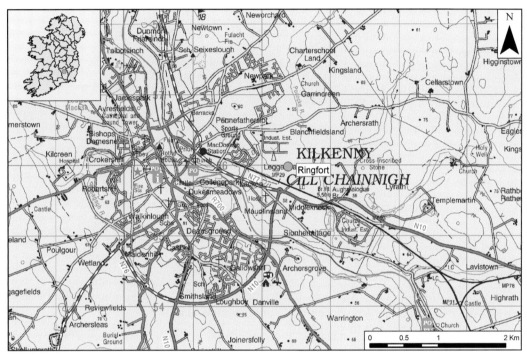

Illus. 1—Location of the Leggetsrath West ringfort, Co. Kilkenny (based on Ordnance Survey Ireland map)

The ringfort at Leggetsrath West was situated to the east of Kilkenny city, on the proposed route of the N77 Kilkenny Ring Road Extension (Illus. 1). The site was identified in a preliminary archaeological assessment of the road corridor as an area of potential archaeological interest. It was the only high point, a naturally occurring hillock, along the route of the proposed road. The site was in an area of rough grazing, which was bound to the east by the Fennell stream and to the west by Hebron Industrial Estate. Archaeological Consultancy Services Ltd carried out investigations in 2004 when the gravel hillock was topsoil stripped, revealing a bivallate (double ditch) ringfort dating from the early historic period (NGR 252383, 155983; height 58.47 m OD; excavation licence no. 04E0661). The ringfort was delimited by two concentric ditches set 4 m apart, with an overall diameter of 54 m. Archaeological excavations were funded by the National Roads Authority through Kilkenny County Council.

Historical and archaeological background

The early historic period in Ireland is dominated by the introduction of Christianity in the fifth century AD. Apart from church sites, the settlement evidence of the period is

43

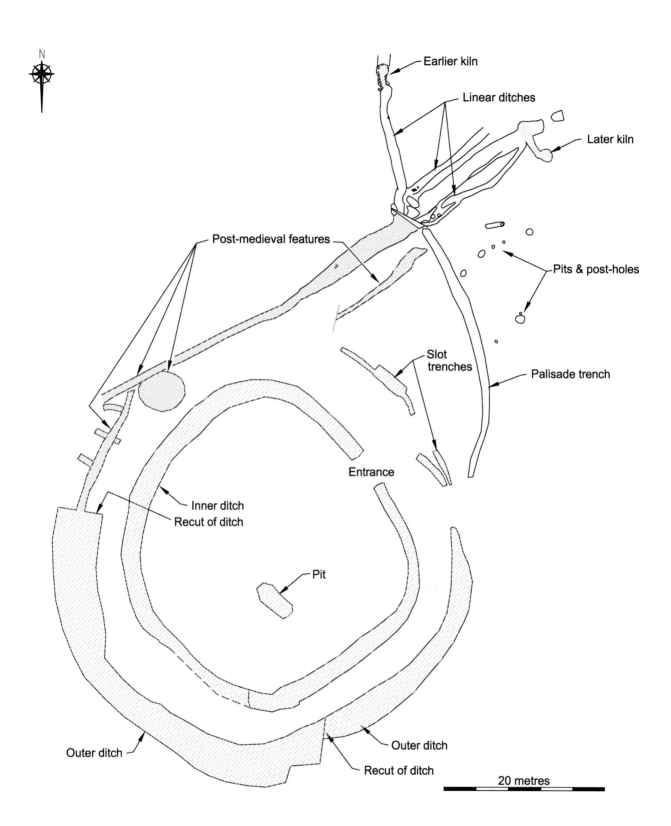

Illus. 2—Plan of excavated features at Leggetsrath West (Archaeological Consultancy Services Ltd)

dominated by two categories of monument: the ringfort and the crannóg. Approximately 1,200 ringforts (also known as raths) are known from County Kilkenny, including one excavated at Loughboy (Record of Monuments and Places [RMP] No. KK019-040), approximately 1.5 km south of Kilkenny city (Cotter 2000). Only one possible crannóg has been recorded in the county, a site identified by aerial photography at Loughmerans (RMP No. KK014-063) to the north of the city. More than 200 church sites have been identified in County Kilkenny. The most famous of these establishments was Cill Chainnigh, or 'the Church of Canice'. The *Annals of Ulster* recorded the death of Canice in AD 599 or 600; however, it cannot be positively ascertained whether Canice or one of his followers founded the monastery in Kilkenny.

The majority of Irish ringforts were probably constructed and occupied during a 300-year period from the beginning of the seventh century to the end of the ninth century (Stout 1997, 29). This view is supported by the fact that the majority of excavated ringforts have provided dates from the second half of the first millennium AD. The site at Leggetsrath West would appear to fall within this time span. The artefacts recovered and the radiocarbon dating place the occupation of the site somewhere between the mid-seventh century and the late ninth century, with it possibly continuing in use into the 11th century.

Excavation results

Inner ditch

The inner ditch (Illus. 2 & 3) measured 34 m east–west by 32 m and enclosed the summit of the hillock. The profile of the inner ditch varied from the east to the west side of the site. On the east side it was U-shaped and shallowest: 0.8 m deep and 1.1 m wide. On the west side the ditch was V-shaped and deeper: 1.4 m deep and 2.3 m wide. It was filled by numerous layers of compact silty clay, loose silty gravel, layers of stone and fine silt. The evidence suggests that the ditch filled in over a short period of time.

Outer ditch

The outer ditch formed a semicircle at the base of the slope, enclosing the east, south and west sides of the site. It was absent on the north side, where the gradient of the slope was sharper. This outer ditch measured 54 m in diameter. The east sector was U-shaped in profile—1 m deep and 1.5 m wide—and was similar in depth to the corresponding segment of the inner ditch. The outer ditch was recut on the south and west sides. The recut was V-shaped—2.3 m deep by 5 m wide—and terminated sharply at each end. The fills recorded from the recut were similar to those in the shallower, eastern part of the ditch, consisting mostly of layers of compact silt and clay, silty gravel, loose stone and fine silts.

Interior

The only archaeological features recorded in the interior of the site were two pits (Illus. 2), one cut into the fill of the other. The earlier and larger pit was 1 m deep, 2 m long (east–west) and 1.7 m wide. It had been truncated at the eastern side by post-medieval gravel quarrying. The pit was filled by several silt and gravel layers. A rudimentary drystone wall-facing, two to three courses high, survived for a length of c. 2 m along the north side. Two post-holes were uncovered, cut into the north and south-west corners of the pit. The

Illus. 3—Aerial photograph of archaeological features at Leggetsrath West (Archaeological Consultancy Services Ltd)

pit may have been used for storage, with posts and the stone walling possibly supporting a roof or canopy. The later pit was 0.6 m in diameter and 0.2 m deep and was cut into the upper fills of the larger pit at its western end.

Entrance

The entrance was represented by a 3 m-wide gap in the inner ditch. It faced north-east and had a commanding view over the surrounding area. There was no evidence of any associated entrance features, such as a gate-house or gate-posts. Nor was there any type of prepared surface leading into or away from the ringfort. The only associated features were external slot-trenches flanking either side of the entrance and respecting the curve of the inner ditch. These were set at a distance of 5 m from the edge of the ditch and extended for a length of 5–6 m. They had a maximum width of 0.6 m and were 0.3 m deep. Both trenches showed evidence of having been recut. The fills of the trenches were similar, comprising silts and gravels with charcoal inclusions. The only direct evidence that the slot-trenches contained upright posts was a shallow post-hole found in the eastern trench.

To the east of the slot-trenches, and respecting the curve of the hill, was a curvilinear ditch, 0.7 m wide with a maximum depth of 0.7 m. It extended for a length of 50 m, terminating sharply at the base of the slope to the north of the ringfort, and was filled by compacted, charcoal-flecked, silty clays. This curvilinear trench may have been used as a palisade trench holding upright timbers, but no evidence of post-holes was found in the base of the trench.

Cereal-drying kilns

A series of intercutting linear field ditches were uncovered at the base of the hillock, to the north-east of the ringfort. They were orientated north-east–south-west and north-west–south-east and had been filled in by compact silt or silty clays with few inclusions. Two of the ditches had cereal-drying kilns built into the upper fills.

The two cereal-drying kilns were uncovered to the north and north-east of the ringfort (Illus. 2), at a distance of c. 40 m. The earlier kiln (radiocarbon-dated to AD 790–1030; see Appendix 1 for details) was keyhole shaped and comprised a single bowl or drying chamber with a connecting flue. It had an overall length of 4.6 m (north–south). Remains of a stone lining survived on the sides of both the drying chamber and the flue, but many of the stones were displaced within the fill. They were large, subrectangular limestone blocks showing evidence of heat fractures. The fire for drying the cereal was lit at the edge of the flue.

The later kiln was radiocarbon-dated to AD 1000–1270 (see Appendix 1). The kiln was 6 m long, orientated north-west–south-east, and comprised two roughly circular bowls with a connecting flue. The larger bowl was used as the drying chamber, and the hot air was directed from the smaller fire-bowl through the flue to the drying chamber (Illus. 4). The smaller fire-bowl showed evidence of *in situ* burning. The remains of a stone lining were found in the flue, comprising a row of angular, heat-shattered limestone blocks set on edge and pressed against the sides of the flue.

A scatter of pits and post- and stake-holes was uncovered to the south of the later kiln, beneath a layer of silt, 0.3–0.4 m deep in places, that had built up around the base of the hill. These features were randomly positioned, forming no definite pattern. Two pits showed evidence of *in situ* burning, suggesting that they may have been used as roasting ovens. Charred cereal grains recovered from these pits were similar to cereals found in the kilns.

Illus. 4—Later cereal-drying kiln radiocarbon-dated to AD 1000–1270 (Archaeological Consultancy Services Ltd)

Post-medieval features

A series of shallow, linear agricultural trenches and a gravel-extraction pit, all dating from the post-medieval period, were uncovered to the west of the ringfort. A linear trench, also of post-medieval date, was identified to the north of the ringfort entrance. It is likely that the linear ditches were part of land drainage practices, draining surface water downslope from the higher ground. The easy access to the gravel on the hill appears to have encouraged attempts to extract gravel from the site for local use.

Palaeoenvironmental evidence

The palaeoenvironmental evidence from the site consisted of charred cereal grains that were concentrated in a few pits and in the two cereal-drying kilns. All of the recovered cereal remains were most likely intended for human consumption and are typical of crops cultivated during the early historic period. The presence of only a small percentage of typical weed seeds in the fills of the kilns suggests that the cereal crop at Leggetsrath West was cleaned before drying. There was a predominance of oats and wheat from the earlier kiln, with barley recovered to a lesser extent. The grain recovered from the later kiln was mainly oats and barley, with a few wheat grains. The charcoal found in the fills of the kilns, pits and post-holes probably represents the wood used for fuel. It is typical of a scrubland environment: a predominance of hazel, with oak, cherry/plum and guilder-rose to a lesser extent. The wood species identifications, along with the shell of a species of land snail found in soil samples from the site, suggest that the immediate environs of the ringfort were shaded by scrubland at the period when the kilns were in use.

The faunal evidence (animal bone) recovered from the ringfort was unexceptional, with cattle, sheep/goat, pig and horse corresponding to the established pattern of animal husbandry for an early historic farmstead. The presence of bird bone is interesting, although only a very small amount was recovered. The species identified included domestic fowl, raven, woodcock, Brent goose and a rook, and all had been previously identified from sites of this period. Fish bone—eel, salmon and trout—recovered from the large pit on the ringfort interior were all of freshwater fish, indicating the exploitation of the nearby River Nore.

Artefacts

The artefact assemblage, although small, produced some very interesting finds. The earliest finds recovered were chert knives, artefacts commonly found throughout the Neolithic and Bronze Age periods. These blades possibly date to later prehistory and are indicative of earlier human activity in the general vicinity of the ringfort. Two of the chert blades, along with a blue glass bead, were from fills of the linear field ditch that had the later of the two kilns built over its upper fills.

Two pottery sherds of Bii amphora ware (mid-fifth/sixth century AD), used to hold wine or olive oil, were recovered from the inner ditch; the first find of imported Mediterranean pottery from this period in south Leinster. The nearest other find of this ware in the south-east was from excavations at Cormac's Chapel, Cashel, Co. Tipperary

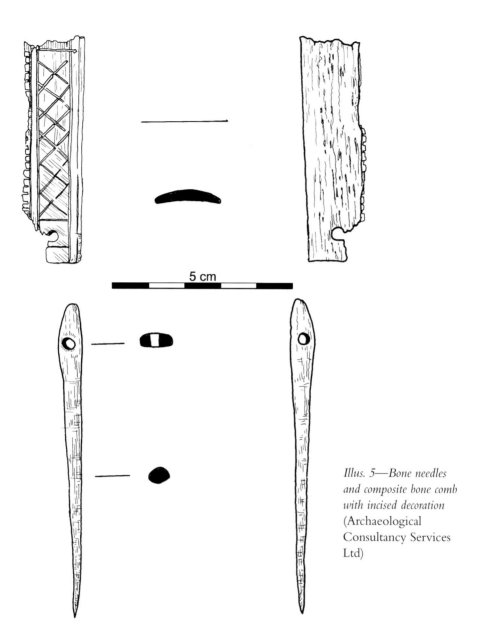

*Illus. 5—Bone needles
and composite bone comb
with incised decoration
(Archaeological
Consultancy Services
Ltd)*

(Hodkinson 1994). Although weathered and residual from the ditch fill, they represent inland trade along the River Nore and are likely to be contemporary with the earliest phase of occupation on the site.

The other artefacts recovered were typical of the assemblages recovered from ringfort excavations in Ireland and included a composite bone comb with incised decoration, a gaming-piece and a loom-weight. The outer ditch produced iron knives and bone needles (Illus. 5). Iron and copper-alloy objects and medieval pottery were also found, but these were unstratified.

The most interesting unstratified find was a cast copper-alloy ring-pin, which was crutch headed and stirrup ringed (Illus. 6). The decoration on the ring-pin consisted of parallel grooves at the middle and ends of the ring. This form of decoration appears to link this ring-pin with ring-pins of the baluster-headed and polyhedral-headed classes, on which this form of decoration is common. By contrast, the form of decoration of the ring of the

Illus. 6—Decorated copper-alloy ring-pin dating to the 11th century AD (Archaeological Consultancy Services Ltd)

Leggetsrath West pin is very rarely employed to decorate the rings of stirrup-ringed pins, on which dot-and-circle motifs are almost universally employed. The pin dates to the 11th century and was made in Dublin. Parallels for this type of decorated pin are known from elsewhere in Ireland, but most examples have been found in Dublin and its immediate hinterland. Most of the pins tend to be found at aristocratic sites such as Ballinderry and Togherstown, Co. Westmeath, and Knowth, Co. Meath. Finds tend to be coastal suggesting that the ringed pins may constitute evidence for maritime trade. However, all but one of the small number of finds from Munster are from ecclesiastical sites, such as Church Island, Valentia; Skellig Michael and Ardfert Cathedral, all in County Kerry, and Liathmore, Co. Tipperary (N Kelly, pers. comm.). This suggests that these pins are high status objects and may have come to Leggetsrath West by means of trade or political or religious interaction in the 11th century, during the last phase of occupation at the ringfort.

Discussion

The features found on the hillock were cut deep into the natural gravel, which was very soft and prone to erosion. The only features recorded from the interior were two pits; there was no trace of occupation layers, nor was evidence for an enclosing bank uncovered. The entire surface of the ringfort, including the area between the two ditches, was rough gravel with medium to large limestone cobbles protruding from the surface. The gravel nature of the site made it very susceptible to erosion, and post-medieval gravel extraction may have hastened the rate of soil erosion.

The fill of the ditches suggested that when they were no longer required they were allowed to backfill quickly. The radiocarbon dates show that the inner ditch was going out of use sometime between AD 610 and AD 780 (see Appendix 1 for details). Because of the lack of suitable organic material from the base of the ditch, the date was obtained from a secondary fill. The dating sample for the outer ditch was taken from the sediment at the base, where the ditch had been recut, and gave a date of AD 690–990 (see Appendix 1). The concentric nature of the two ditches and the overlap in dating suggest that their construction was contemporaneous. However, it is possible that the site was extended sometime between the seventh and the eighth century by backfilling the inner ditch, a practice not uncommon in ringforts (Monk 1998, 41). A recut was then made to the outer ditch on the least defensive part of the enclosure and may represent a period in the eighth century when deeper defences were required.

The entrance to the site was a simple causeway formed by an unexcavated gap in the inner ditch. It faced north, taking advantage of the commanding view over the north-east route into the early ecclesiastical settlement at Kilkenny. The entrance was flanked by a probable defensive feature consisting of slot-trenches that may have held timber uprights. A possible palisade trench was found extending the length of the north slope, on the east side of the site, which may also have had a defensive role.

To the north of the site associated peripheral activity was uncovered downslope of the ringfort. The features survived in this area because they were sealed by a deep deposit of silt or hill-wash from upslope. The linear field ditches may represent part of the division of the infield, where small fields tend to radiate from ringforts and were used for grazing and cultivation, often with a kiln for cereal drying built into them (Kelly 1998, 368). The cereal-drying kilns built over the ditches suggest that the field ditches are either contemporary with or earlier than the occupation of the ringfort. It is not uncommon to uncover elements of an earlier field system comprising linear ditches pre-dating ringforts. The earlier of the two kilns has been dated to AD 790–1030 (Appendix 1), well within the known occupation period of Irish ringforts. The later kiln was dated to AD 1000–1270 (Appendix 1). This may place its use at the end of the occupation phase of the ringfort or when the ringfort was out of use but occupation still continued in the vicinity.

The ringfort at Leggetsrath West was clearly of some importance throughout its occupation. Its setting in the landscape is quite deliberate and would have made it prominent and perhaps imposing to some extent. Moreover, the ringfort was situated at the junction of two major early medieval routeways—an east–west routeway from Leinster to Munster at the foot of the Castlecomer plateau and a north–south routeway along the River Nore. As such, a good deal of effort went into defending the site. However, its significance is perhaps best represented by two of the high-status artefacts recovered during the excavation—the sherds of Mediterranean Bii amphora ware and the copper-alloy ring-pin. These finds represent the earliest and latest phases of occupation on the site and clearly indicate the significance of the ringfort over a number of centuries and the extent of trade in luxury items in the region during this period.

Acknowledgements

The author wishes to thank James Eogan, project archaeologist, Tramore House Regional Design Office, and Trevor Mbwebwe, WS Akins Ireland Ltd, who contributed to the project in a variety of ways. Particular thanks to the excavation crew and the staff of Archaeological Consultancy Services Ltd for their dedication and hard work throughout the project. Thanks also to the following for specialist analysis: Ian Doyle (medieval pottery); Ned Kelly (ring-pin); Dr Eiméar Nelis (lithics); Fiona Beglane and Sheila Hamilton-Dyer (animal

Settlement, Industry and Ritual

52

bones); Orni Akeret, Deborah Jacques and John Carrott of Palaeoecology Research Services (plant remains) and Beta Analytic, Florida, who conducted the radiocarbon dating. Final thanks to Adrian Kenny for the conservation of the metal artefacts and to John Murphy for the illustrations.

6. Archaeological investigation of a souterrain at Tateetra, Dundalk, County Louth

Avril Hayes

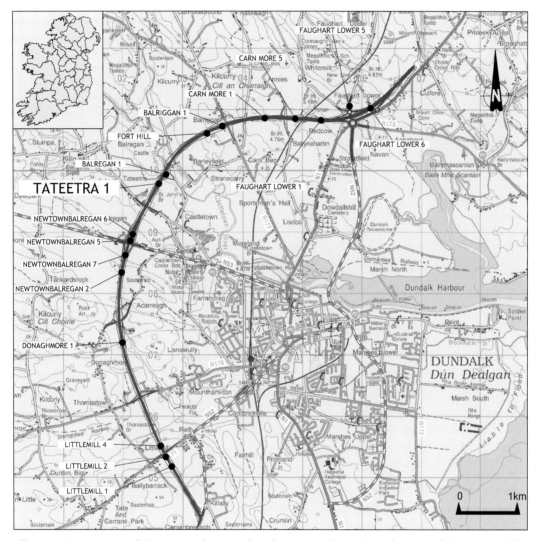

Illus. 1—Location map of Tateetra in relation to the other excavated sites along the route of the M1 Dundalk Western Bypass (Meath County Council National Roads Design Office, based on the Ordnance Survey Ireland map)

The souterrain at Tateetra was situated north-west of Dundalk, Co. Louth, and south of the Castletown River in an area of gently undulating topography (Illus. 1 & 2). The site (NGR 302587, 309824; height 10 m OD; ministerial direction no. A010/001) was partly excavated by Aegis Archaeology Ltd between September and December 2004 on behalf of Celtic Roads Dundalk Group, as part of a public-private partnership with the National Roads Authority before construction of the M1 Dundalk Western Bypass. This paper presents a provisional interpretation of the site. A full discussion of the archaeological findings will be published after completion of the post-excavation analysis.

Illus. 2—Aerial view of the souterrain at Tateetra, from the south-west (Aegis Archaeology Ltd)

The souterrain was discovered during works along the north-western side of the proposed road, under the west side of an already constructed road embankment when a drainage trench cut through the south side of a chamber. As this represented a possible danger to the new road (through future collapse) the road embankment was removed, exposing 30 m of the souterrain, with a further 10 m outside of the road corridor. What initially appeared to be the entrance to the souterrain was exposed, but it was quickly seen that the excavation area needed to be extended. Another large section of the new embankment was removed, revealing an additional 30 m-long section of the souterrain. A detailed survey of the structure was undertaken by Gridpoint Solutions Ltd using laser scanning equipment, before and after the removal of the capstones. (The use of this new technology meant that planning by hand was kept to a minimum.) On foot of the excavation the walls were left *in situ*, the passages were filled with gravel and the majority of the capstones were replaced. Nine capstones, three of which were decorated, were retained by Dundalk Museum.

The souterrain was roughly U-shaped in plan. It was drystone built and measured approximately 70 m in total length, incorporating two chambers, four galleries or long passages, two doorways featuring bolt-holes, a drop-hole, a step, three sumps/wells, a pit, a wall niche and an air-vent (Illus. 3).[1] No evidence of an associated settlement was found

---

[1] An alternative interpretation is that the structures at Tateetra represent not one but two souterrains (Roycroft 2005, 76)—Eds.

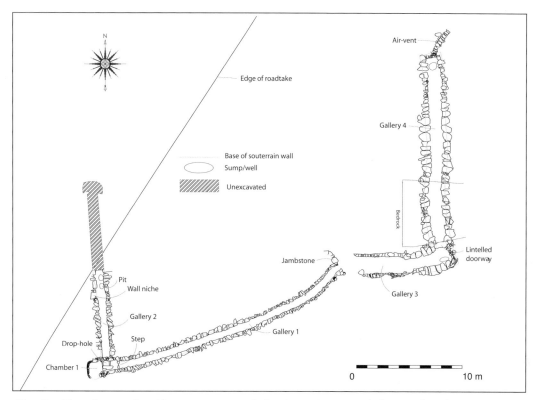

Illus. 3—Plan of souterrain with capstones removed, showing main structural elements (based on a survey by Gridpoint Solutions Ltd)

Illus. 4—View of Chamber 1, drop-hole providing access to Gallery 2 and step at west end of Gallery 1 (Aegis Archaeology Ltd)

during the excavation, but it is most probably situated beyond the limit of excavation. Alternatively, centuries of agricultural activity may have destroyed the settlement that was once associated with the souterrain at Tateetra.

All of the souterrain walls were drystone built and consisted of roughly coursed shale overlying a basal foundation course of large stones set on edge. The upper courses of the walls were slightly corbelled. (The souterrain was constructed by firstly excavating trenches for the galleries and chambers. The walls would then have been inserted, each section roofed with capstones and the whole structure covered with earth.) Gallery 1 consisted of a small, restricted passage with an oval chamber and a drop-hole at its eastern end (Illus. 4). (A drop-hole is a defensive feature that would have made access difficult for intruders as they would have had to climb up or down to the next section of the souterrain, leaving themselves open to attack.) This drop-hole provided access to Gallery 2, another restricted passage. Gallery 2 was not fully investigated as an 8 m portion of the gallery lay outside the area affected by the road scheme. However, it appeared to terminate in a sub-circular chamber to the north, which was heavily collapsed. Galleries 3 and 4 consisted of larger, less restricted passages, with a lintelled doorway and jambs giving access to Gallery 4. Gallery 3 was badly disturbed at its western end. Most of its length was filled in, and a number of collapsed capstones were found in the passage. Gallery 4 terminated to the north with an air-vent feature.

Galleries 1 and 2 and Chamber 1 were smaller than Galleries 3 and 4 (Illus. 5 & 6). It is unknown whether this represents two phases of construction as the west end of Gallery 3 was disturbed. It would appear from a bracing socket at the east end of Gallery 1 (Illus. 7) that all of the galleries were in use at the same time, as the associated doorway gave access to Galleries 3 and 1. (Similar bracing sockets were noted at the lintelled doorway into Gallery 4 [Illus. 8].) The entrance to the souterrain may have been situated in this area, but evidence of this has been obscured. Alternatively, the souterrain entrance may lie beyond the area affected by the road scheme, in the unexcavated, northern end of Gallery 2.

Illus. 5—View inside Gallery 1 from the east, showing restrictive size (Aegis Archaeology Ltd)

Illus. 6—View inside Gallery 4 from the south, showing less restrictive size (Aegis Archaeology Ltd)

Artefacts

The artefacts recovered from the excavation appear to be consistent with the general date of souterrains in Ireland, which is from the latter half of the first millennium to the early part of the second millennium AD. A copper-alloy stick-pin (late 11th to mid-13th century in date) was found in the floor surface at the east end of Gallery 1, near the entrance. A perforated white bead was recovered from the packing over Gallery 3. There are eight examples of beads from souterrains in Ireland, made from blue glass, amber, polished stone and horse tooth, with a general date of the latter centuries of the first millennium AD (Clinton 2001, 80). Fragments of pottery from a single pot were recovered from the floor of Gallery 2. The pot is decorated and has a 'stamped' rosette. It appears to be an example of the coarse, unglazed domestic pottery known as Souterrain Ware. Souterrain Ware dates from the seventh to the 12th century, and the decoration on the pot places it at the later end of the sequence (S Zajac, pers. comm.).

Two cross-inscribed slabs had been reused as capstones over Gallery 4 at Tateetra. One slab contained five equal-armed crosses on five different faces of the stone (Illus. 9) and is tentatively identified as an altar pillar (T Ó Carragáin, pers. comm.). The second slab was a large stone with a small Latin cross on its underside. There is a theory (O'Rahilly 1946; Warner 1980) that the reuse of cross-slabs in the building of souterrains was intended to ward off the evil associated with being underground. While this possibility cannot be ruled out, it should be noted that at Tateetra none of the crosses on the slabs were clearly visible inside the souterrain. Neither were they placed at strategic locations, such as chambers or

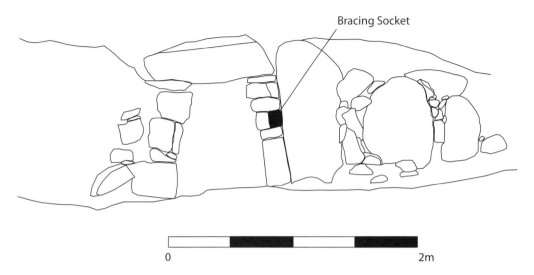

Bracing Socket

0   2m

Illus. 7—East-facing elevation drawing showing entrance to Gallery 1 at the east (Gridpoint Solutions Ltd)

Illus. 8—Bolt-holes and bracing sockets on western door-jamb and wall of lintelled doorway into Gallery 4 (Aegis Archaeology Ltd)

entrances. In the case of Tateetra it would appear that the crosses may not have been important to the builders.

A reused stone featuring megalithic art (i.e. the abstract geometric art associated with Neolithic tombs) was employed as the final capstone at the north end of Gallery 4. It was set on edge over the souterrain, with the decorated surface facing north. The decoration consisted, for the most part, of incised lozenge motifs. The decorated face of the stone was damaged, and it was obvious that the weathered surface had broken off in places. The slab

Illus. 9—Cross-inscribed stone, possibly a reused altar pillar, overlying Gallery 4 (Aegis Archaeology Ltd)

had possibly been taken from the site of an archaeological complex, no longer extant, across the Castletown River to the north in the townland of Balregan. This complex (Record of Monuments and Places No. LH007-001) incorporates the sites of two standing stones, two possible cairns, a possible stone alignment and the site of a stone pair. The occurrence of the megalithic art at Tateetra appears to be more opportunistic than deliberate, as the face containing the decoration was completely obscured by fill and the art was noted only when the capstone was removed (Illus. 10).

Function

There are two major theories on the function of souterrains in Ireland—refuge and storage. The storage explanation has been attributed to less complex souterrains with ramped or stepped entrances (Clinton 2001, 105). The easily accessible nature of some souterrains in south-east Scotland prompted Warner (1979, 129) to support the storage view—as these are typically wide and broad with gently sloping entrances—but he noted that it was an inadequate explanation with regard to Irish souterrains. Limbert (1996, 259) saw souterrains as evidence of an increasing reliance on agriculture, at the expense of animal husbandry, and believed that they were used for storing cereals and other produce.

Warner (1980, 96) saw the ringfort and souterrain as a response to a specific problem within a particular socio-economic structure. He believed that warring Irish tribes had stabilised somewhat by the eighth century, allowing the construction of permanent

Illus. 10—Capstone from the north end of Gallery 4 featuring megalithic art (Aegis Archaeology Ltd)

habitation sites (ringforts and open settlements). But local raids still occurred, and this necessitated the retention of the initial line of defence, the ringfort, and the creation of a secondary defence for the 'non-combatant inhabitants', the souterrain. Buckley (1986) suggested that concentrations of souterrains reflect the centres of tribal power, such as the Dál Riata in north Antrim and north-east Derry (i.e. the kingship of the Ulaid) and suggested—*contra* Warner—that they reflect an increased need for defence as the tribes still contested control.

From the available literature it is obvious that the function of souterrains should be discussed on a site-by-site basis, drawing on structural elements particular to the souterrain. It is in this regard that a refuge function has been attributed to the souterrain at Tateetra. There are a number of structural elements in support of this view. Although unrestrictive in size, the presence of an air-vent at the end of Gallery 4 would suggest that there was a supply of air for occupants who had locked themselves into the gallery. Probably the most obvious elements are associated with the doorways to the east of Gallery 1 and in Gallery 4. In both cases the locations of the bracing sockets—and in Gallery 4 the bolt-holes—are defensive in nature. The doors would have been secured from the interior of the souterrain. A second defensive element would have been the restrictive size of Galleries 1 and 2. There is no standing headroom in either of the passages, and so movement would have been in a crouched position. Equally, the presence of a drop-hole at the west end of Gallery 1, giving access to Gallery 2, would not have been conducive to free movement within the souterrain. If there is an entrance to the souterrain from the unexcavated end of Gallery 2, the drop-hole would have been easily defended by occupants of Gallery 1. If the entrance to the souterrain was from Gallery 1, the drop-hole would still have provided an impediment to any intruders.

The presence of a wall niche and pit in Gallery 2 suggests a secondary storage function for the souterrain, although it is more likely that these features were used during a period of refuge. The restrictive nature of Gallery 2 and the fact that it may have been entered from Gallery 1 through the drop-hole would rule out a primary storage function, as this would have been an awkward way to gain access to stored goods. If, however, access to the pit and niche was from the north end of Gallery 2, they are positioned too far along the gallery to have been convenient.

Conclusion

The incorporation of cross-inscribed slabs and the associated finds may indicate a construction date in the late first millennium AD, with continued use into the early second millennium. The souterrain appears to have been constructed using locally available stone, except for the granite slabs used in the doorways. The nearby Cooley Mountains are the closest source of granite in the area. The decorated stones may have been taken from nearby sites (for example, the archaeological complex at Balregan), and their reuse in the souterrain appears to represent opportunistic recycling rather than deliberate selection for ritual or symbolic reasons. The finds appear to be consistent with the general date of souterrains in Ireland—the latter half of the first millennium to the early part of the second millennium. No evidence of an associated settlement was found during the excavation, but one surely existed and may yet be identified beyond the limit of excavation. Structural aspects of the souterrain, most notably its restrictive nature and the interior locking arrangement employed at doorways, indicate a primary function of refuge.

Acknowledgements

The excavation was funded by Celtic Roads Group Dundalk. Line drawings were produced by Gridpoint Solutions Ltd. The writer thanks the excavation team and staff of Aegis Archaeology Ltd. The project archaeologist on the M1 Dundalk Western Bypass was Niall Roycroft, Meath County Council National Roads Design Office.

7. Excavation of an early medieval 'plectrum-shaped' enclosure at Newtown, County Limerick

Frank Coyne

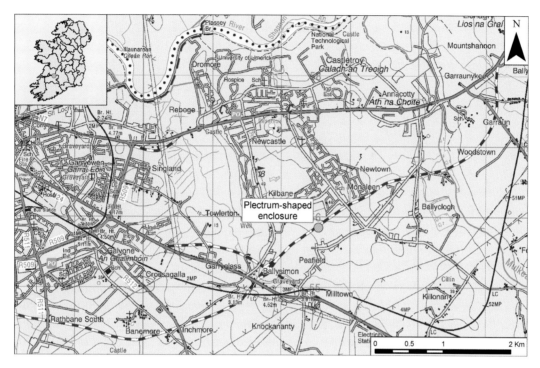

Illus. 1—Location of site at Newtown, Co. Limerick (based on the Ordnance Survey Ireland map)

The site at Newtown was first identified in 2001 during a large-scale, pre-construction ploughing and test-trenching project before construction of the Limerick Southern Ring Road Phase I. There was no trace of the archaeological features above the ground before investigation. The site was to the east of Limerick city (Illus. 1), in the townland of Newtown (NGR 162550, 155850; height 30 m OD; excavation licence no. 01E0214). The excavation was funded by the National Roads Authority, through Limerick County Council.

Two distinct phases of activity were identified at this site: a prehistoric Bronze Age phase represented by two structures, interpreted as houses, and a cemetery containing quantities of funerary pottery; and a subsequent reuse of the site in the early medieval period (Illus. 2). This paper concentrates on the early medieval phase of activity. This was represented by a 'plectrum-shaped' enclosure (identified as Newtown A) containing a figure-of-eight structure, which was partly constructed on top of the Bronze Age cemetery. (The two Bronze Age houses were situated to the north of the plectrum-shaped enclosure.) Part of a possible second enclosure (identified as Newtown E) was also excavated. This extended beyond the area affected by the road scheme, and so its full extent could not be ascertained. It was situated to the west of the plectrum-shaped enclosure.

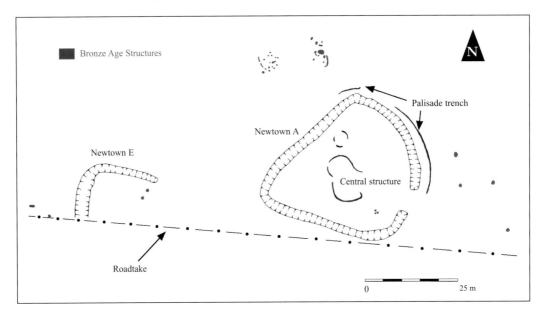

Illus. 2—Plan of excavated features at Newtown (Aegis Archaeology Ltd)

The plectrum-shaped enclosure (Newtown A)

Newtown A was not visible before the pre-development ploughing programme. (The aim of the ploughing was to bring to light any traces of archaeological activity that may have been in or beneath the ploughsoil.) Originally, only the figure-of-eight structure was noted during test trenching. Topsoil stripping around the structure revealed that it was part of a larger complex and was in fact contained within a larger plectrum-shaped enclosure. (Coyne & Collins [2003] coined the term 'plectrum-shaped' in an earlier article on this site. A plectrum is used for plucking or strumming stringed instruments and is generally triangular or sub-triangular in shape.) This enclosure had a maximum width of more than 50 m, with a single, 5 m-wide causewayed entrance to the east (Illus. 3). The enclosing ditch was V-shaped in profile and averaged 3 m in width. This ditch was partly surrounded on its eastern and northern sides by a narrow trench, interpreted as an external palisade slot-trench. All features were uncovered immediately below the topsoil, with very little intercutting of features.

Entrance

The entrance consisted of a causeway formed by a 5 m-wide undug portion of the ditch and was revetted in places by stone facing. A series of post-holes and a slot-trench, uncovered immediately inside the entranceway, may all have been part of a gatehouse. Immediately inside the entrance was an area of cobbling associated with the post-holes. This layer displayed evidence of two different phases. A layer of small, angular cobbles had been partly covered by a layer of larger cobbles, which suggests an attempt at repairing or resurfacing the entrance area, probably as the surface wore away through use.

Interior

The centre of the enclosure was dominated by the figure-of-eight structure. A circular structure, 5 m in diameter, was situated NNW of this but had been severely truncated by

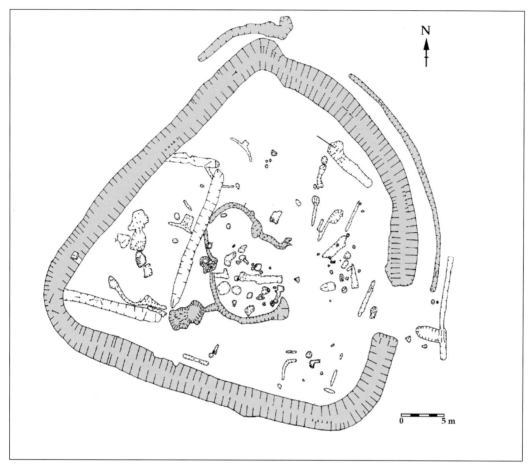

Illus. 3—Plan of plectrum-shaped enclosure (Newtown A) with figure-of-eight building in interior (Aegis Archaeology Ltd)

later drainage activity. Unfortunately, no dating evidence was recovered from this structure. The remainder of the interior contained various linear features and pits.

A series of linear features, some very shallow, were excavated in the eastern half of the interior in a sandy portion of the site. No finds or dating evidence was recovered from these features, and it is likely that some of these, on the basis of their irregular shape, may be the remains of rabbit burrows. A long, narrow, linear feature was also excavated to the north of these features, but its date or function remains unknown.

A series of drains were recorded in the western half of the interior. The largest was a north–south-running feature, probably the remains of a field drain, which produced modern pottery and glass. Various pit features were found to the west of the central structure, some substantial. They had no stratigraphic relationship with each other, however, and did not contain any datable material or artefacts, and so their precise function remains unknown. A large pit was situated to the south-west of the central structure, from which a flint blade was recovered.

Figure-of-eight structure

The most intensive evidence of activity within the enclosure was found at its centre, where the figure-of-eight-shaped building was situated. This measured 11 m internally

Illus. 4—Figure-of-eight building, from the north (Aegis Archaeology Ltd)

north–south by a maximum of 9 m (Illus. 3 & 4). There were a large number of pits and post-holes in the southern part of the interior of this structure, which was partly delineated by a shallow, east–west, linear trench.

The figure-of-eight building may have been a combination or amalgamation of two semicircular structures. It is similar in ground plan, although not in construction technique, to structures A–D at the early medieval ecclesiastical site at Reask, Co. Kerry, which were conjoined, circular stone huts (Fanning 1981, 91–2). Similar structures have been found at other early medieval sites. The most notable parallel is that from Deer Park Farms, Co. Antrim (Mallory & McNeill 1991, 191, figs 6–12), where more than 30 houses were found (Lynn 1987), although only three or four were occupied at any one time. The houses had many of the features described in the law tracts as that of a farmer of the lowest independent grade (*ocaire*), including houses conjoined in a figure-of-eight shape (Stout 2000, 92).

A small but interesting range of artefacts was recovered (Illus. 5). A green glass bead with yellow paste herringbone decoration was recovered from the fill of the linear trench, and a shallow pit north of this trench produced a dark blue glass bead. The slot-trench for the structure produced part of a glass armlet with white decoration, an iron knife and a socketed iron implement, which was too corroded to be positively identified. The slot-trench on the northern side of the structure produced a flint scraper, some horse teeth and the top of an adult human skull (aged about 30 years but of indeterminate sex). A hone stone was also

Illus. 5—Glass beads, glass armlet and iron knife (Aegis Archaeology Ltd)

Illus. 6—Human skull fragment in the foundation trench of the figure-of-eight building, from the west (Aegis Archaeology Ltd)

recovered from the central post-hole of the figure-of-eight building. Again, very little stratigraphic evidence was encountered, and no distinct layers of occupation were noted.

The most intriguing finds are undoubtedly the human skull fragment (Illus. 6), the flint scraper and the horse teeth. These appear to have been deposited deliberately, presumably a foundation deposit during the construction of the building. If this is the case, the occupants of this site may have retained some pagan beliefs, perhaps when the majority of people were converting to Christianity. This deposition had all the appearance of a pagan rite and, when coupled with the unusual shape of the enclosure itself, raises many intriguing questions about the exact nature of this site.

Dating

Suitable samples from several features were sent for radiocarbon dating (see Appendix 1 for details). Charcoal from the slot-trench of the central building yielded a date of AD 700–1015 (Beta-182313). The central post-hole of this building produced a date of AD 795–1280 (Beta-182314), from what appears to be the remains of an oak post. The basal fill of the enclosing ditch was dated to AD 795–1030 (Beta-182317). Charcoal from an upper fill, which may date the final levelling of the site, produced a date of AD 1010–1300 (Beta-182323).

The radiocarbon determinations and the artefact assemblage suggest that the main concentration of activity on the site dates to the latter part of the first millennium, within the early medieval period. The most diagnostic finds are the two glass beads and the portion of the blue glass armlet. The most impressive of the glass beads is the green bead with herringbone decoration in yellow paste or enamel. A similar bead was found at Reask, Co. Kerry. This type of bead is of Irish manufacture and dates to the second half of the first millennium AD (Fanning 1981, 121). Blue glass beads are ubiquitous in Irish archaeology and almost impossible to date in isolation; they may date from the Bronze Age through to the early medieval period (Warner & Meighan 1994, 52).

The portion of the blue glass armlet is of the highest quality and can be paralleled with finds from elsewhere in Ireland. For example, a comparable armlet was found at the royal crannóg of Lagore, Co. Meath (Eogan 2000, 79), and another, almost identical, example from Ireland is housed in the National Museum of Denmark (Eogan 1991, 165). The Newtown armlet conforms to Carroll's (2001, 105) Class 1 bangle. She suggested that the reason for the production of luxury glass items on secular sites may have been connected with the importance of gift giving and reciprocity in early medieval Ireland, and this may explain the discovery of bangles and huge numbers of glass beads on high-status sites from the seventh to the 10th century (ibid., 107).

Lagore crannóg had a period of use from the seventh to the 10th century, and the blue glass armlet presumably dates from this period. However, it is worth noting that items of value may have had a long period of use and may have been retained as treasured heirlooms. The armlet may have been in circulation for a considerable period of time until being finally lost or deposited in the ground. Geographically, the closest parallel for the Newtown armlet was found during the excavations of a cashel at Carraig Aille II, Lough Gur, Co. Limerick (ibid., 113; Ó Ríordáin 1949).

Illus. 7—Aerial photograph of Newtown A, from the west (Aegis Archaeology Ltd)

Newtown E

This site was some 25 m to the west of the plectrum-shaped enclosure (Newtown A) and took the form of what appeared to be another sub-triangular ditch (Illus. 8). No diagnostic find was recovered from the fill of this ditch, nor was any datable charcoal retrieved. The eastern side of this ditch feature was truncated by a substantial, north–south-orientated field boundary and extended to the south beyond the area affected by the road scheme. The field boundary was substantial and had its own deep ditch on its eastern side. It is likely to have obliterated the enclosure ditch and may have incorporated part of it. It was therefore impossible to ascertain its true shape through excavation. Nonetheless, it might be speculated that this possible enclosure was part of another plectrum-shaped enclosure.

Illus. 8—Aerial photograph of Newtown E, from the north-east (Aegis Archaeology Ltd)

Newtown A: what is the site?

It would be wrong to classify this plectrum-shaped enclosure as a ringfort, as this would be to deny the enclosure's morphology. It has an entrance on its eastern side, probably to shelter it from the prevailing winds (Stout 1997, 18), and both the artefacts and the radiocarbon samples would seem to date the main activity on-site to about the 8th to the 11th century AD. The earliest dates fall within the accepted date range for the use of ringforts: from the beginning of the seventh century to the end of the ninth century (ibid., 30). However, for its size, there is an almost complete absence of animal bone and general occupation evidence from the site, which implies that it may not have had a settlement function. Furthermore, despite the comparable date range, Newtown A does not fit into the present classification of ringforts. For example, Stout (2003) defines ringforts as 'the protected farmsteads of the Early Historic Period, consisting of a roughly circular space, surrounded by a bank and outer fosse, or simply by a rampart of stone. Also known as *ráth*, *dún*, *lios*, rath and fort, with stone examples called cashel (*caiseal*) or caher (*cathair*).' Most ringforts are fairly circular, and it has been suggested that each new ringfort was laid out using a measuring line pivoted from a central stake (Stout 1997, 14).

If not a ringfort, then what exactly is Newtown A? The origin of ringforts is a vexed question in Irish archaeology. Did they come into use in the Iron Age, or were they an early medieval innovation (Limbert 1996; Edwards 1990, 17; O'Kelly 1951)? Indeed, it has been pointed out in various sources that the term 'ringfort' is a misnomer, and there is some degree of disagreement about their effectiveness in a defensive situation. This leads to the question of whether the term 'fort' should be applied to the monument type at all (Limbert 1996, 252).

As tens of thousands of ringforts were constructed, after the same fashion, in the space of a few hundred years, shape must have been an important consideration for the builders (Stout 1997, 24). Following on from this, can archaeologists then differentiate between ringforts and other oddly shaped enclosures? Do they have a different genesis from each other, and do they display a difference in status? Certainly the finds from Newtown seem to indicate that this site was occupied by a high-status group.

It appears that the type of enclosure represented at Newtown is present in the archaeological landscape but hidden in the archaeological record. In the absence of a clearly defined typology, they have been classified as ringforts or enclosures. The published archaeological inventories for various counties in Ireland show enclosures that are indeed plectrum-shaped, or non-circular at the very least. Aerial reconnaissance, as well as field survey, also appears to be shedding light on unusual, previously unrecorded, enclosures. Gillian Barrett's work in Counties Carlow and Kildare has highlighted several of these unusually shaped enclosures, some of which might be described as plectrum-shaped, although this term is not used (Barrett 2002). Perhaps one important reason that these sites are not commonly identified through field survey is that their banks and ditches may not have been substantial and may therefore have been easily levelled.

Two sites that have been excavated recently, although they do not appear to conform exactly to the 'plectrum shape', still have an unusual morphology: Killickaweeny, Co. Kildare (Walsh & Harrison 2003), and Balriggan, Co. Louth (Delaney & Roycroft 2003). A third example has been discovered recently in County Clare (Hull & Taylor 2005, 38). All of these sites bear similarities to the Newtown enclosure, although they have been described initially as 'heart-shaped' elsewhere (Delaney & Walsh 2004). The artefacts recovered are generally all of high quality, which would suggest wealthy occupants, and their dating is of similar range.

Conclusions

This site at Newtown A has some shared characteristics with ringforts. Central structures are found in ringforts; the positioning of the entrance is not unusual; and the artefactual and dating evidence dates the site to the early medieval period. In the absence of similar excavated sites, the discussion of the site remains somewhat in the realms of speculation. In conclusion, excavation of this site at Newtown has served to alert us to the diversity of archaeological sites that await discovery in the landscape. The discovery of a plectrum-shaped enclosure demonstrates that there must surely have been a greater variety of sites in use in the early medieval period in Ireland than has been recognised to date.

Acknowledgements

Thanks to Linda G Lynch for identification of the human remains and to Ellen OCarroll for identification of the charcoal. Thanks also to the Aegis Archaeology Ltd excavation team: Fran Wilkinson, Denis Healy, Aidan Cahill, Caoimhe Ní Tobín, Dawn Gooney, Ivan Pawle, Bruce Sutton, Tony Cummins, Mary Liz McCarthy, Bernie Doherty, Brian Fitzgerald, Jim Kelly and Stephen Collins.

8. Through the mill—excavation of an early medieval settlement at Raystown, County Meath

Matthew Seaver

On a long, low ridge in the small townland of Raystown, Co. Meath, west of what is now Ashbourne, people began burying their dead in an enclosed cemetery in the early fifth century AD. This place was to endure for at least 600 years as a large farming settlement. The building and maintenance of a remarkable series of watermills and watercourses and the production of cereals defined the lives of generations before the site became disused sometime in the 11th or 12th century.

Excavations in 2004 and 2005 by Cultural Resource Development Services Ltd (CRDS Ltd) in the road corridor of the N2 Finglas–Ashbourne road scheme uncovered the extensive remains of this settlement (NGR 304976, 251474; height 65–71 m OD; excavation licence no. 03E1229 extension; ministerial direction no. A011). This route bypasses the growing town of Ashbourne. Raystown was one of 20 sites (Illus. 1) excavated on behalf of the National Roads Authority and Meath County Council (see FitzGerald, this volume). This paper aims to outline the results of the excavation of this unique site and to illustrate its potential to add to our knowledge of early medieval Ireland.

Discovery

The site is in the barony and parish of Ratoath, between the towns of Ashbourne and Ratoath. It is situated c. 350 m north of the east–west road between Swords and Ashbourne. This was a medieval communications route from Dublin to Trim and was used by King John in 1185 (Orpen 1911, 247). The importance of the road declined after the construction of the north–south turnpike road in the 18th century, which became known as the N2. The site is centred on a north–south ridge in an area of relatively low-lying land, criss-crossed by numerous streams (Illus. 2). It is bordered to the east by a stream, which farther north enters the Broad Meadow River, and to the west by low-lying, sometimes waterlogged, ground. This leaves the site bounded on three sides by water. The site was discovered by GSB Prospection Ltd during an extensive pre-development geophysical survey of selected areas in 2002. The survey suggested that the site, which extended beyond the road corridor, covered an area measuring at least 160 m east–west by 250 m. Trial trenching and initial excavation by Judith Carroll Network Archaeology Ltd in 2003 confirmed the presence of a significant early medieval site. The entire area within the road corridor, approximately one-third of the overall site, was subsequently excavated by CRDS Ltd.

History and landscape

It is important to place the site within its contemporary early medieval landscape: it lay in the ancient kingdom of Brega and in the sub-kingdom of Deisceart Breg (Southern Brega). This important early kingdom, which may have evolved in the seventh century, was later

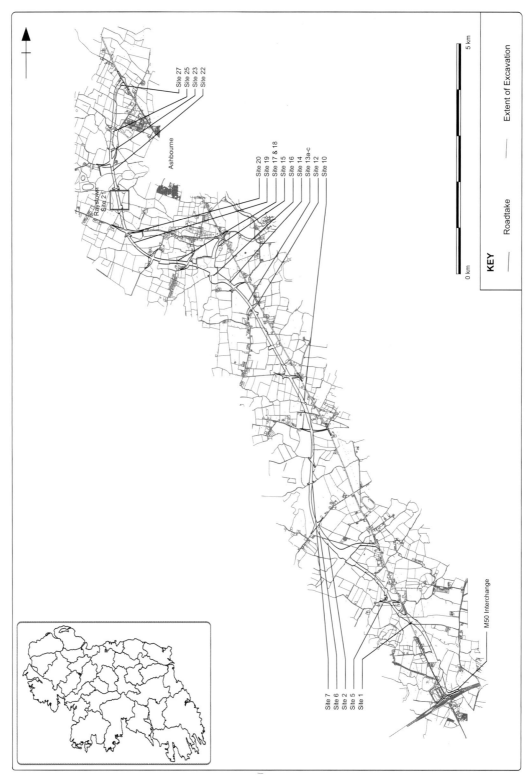

Illus. 1—Location map showing Raystown (Site 21) and other sites identified on the route of the N2 Finglas–Ashbourne road scheme (CRDS Ltd, based on Ordnance Survey Ireland map)

incorporated into the expanding kingdom of Mide (Charles-Edwards 2000, 234; Bhreathnach 1999, 3). Southern Brega was in turn divided into a number of smaller territories, whose extents correspond with the later barony boundaries. The barony of Ratoath relates to the area held by the Mac Gilla Sechnaill (Clann Chernaig Sotail), a family of the Southern Uí Néill dynasty.

In the immediate area the physical remains of this period survive both as sites listed in the Record of Monuments and Places (RMP) and as sites discovered through archaeological excavation. The kingship of Brega was centred on the royal stronghold at Lagore crannóg, an artificial island in a lake close to Dunshaughlin, excavated in the 1930s. Christianity was introduced to the area in the fifth century, and missionaries linked to St Patrick founded churches at Dunshaughlin (RMP No. ME044-003), Trevet (ME038-017) and Kilbrew (ME038-023). Raystown is close to early church sites at Donaghmore (ME045-008) and Killegland (ME045-002 & -003). Both sites incorporate underground passages known as souterrains. Another souterrain is known from Baltrasna (ME045-022-06). Another church site of unknown, but at least medieval, date can be found at Cookstown bridge (ME045-001). (All of the sites noted above are 1–9 km from the Raystown site.)

Ringforts, the ubiquitous monuments of the period, are relatively sparse in the area. These were circular, ditched farmstead enclosures, often set within their own fields. Owing to ploughing and clearance, many of these monuments have been levelled and are identifiable only through aerial/geophysical survey, careful observation of field patterns, accidental discovery or archaeological excavation. Probable examples can be found at Killegland, and a further enclosure (Site 22) in the same townland may also be a ringfort. The N2 realigned route passes close to the latter site, and a number of kilns and furnaces were excavated nearby and are likely to be late Iron Age/early medieval in date. (Site 22 was excavated by Laurence McGowan under excavation licence no. 03E1327.) Part of another large ringfort (Site 25) was also excavated on the route at Cookstown. (Site 25 was excavated by Richard Clutterbuck under excavation licence no. 03E1252.)

The excavated site

The excavations at Raystown uncovered a burial ground enclosed by a series of concentric ditches, as well as two areas of domestic activity, one of which incorporated two souterrains. Outside this core area were a large number of radiating boundary and drainage ditches, clusters of cereal-drying kilns and the remains of at least eight watermills and the large watercourses that powered them (Illus. 3 & 4).

Secrets from the grave
The burial ground at Raystown was centred on the top of a ridge, and approximately half of it was within the road corridor. There was no excavated evidence for an entrance, but geophysical survey suggests that this was on the western edge, beyond the road corridor. A further concentric enclosure, measuring 50 m across, was defined by a more substantial ditch, which had been recut on numerous occasions.

The presence of a burial ground always makes the actions of humans in the past seem more tangible, and excavations here recovered 93 articulated burials. Grave-digging and

Illus. 2—Aerial photograph of Raystown with topographical contours at 1 m intervals (white lines) and geophysical survey data (blue lines) (CRDS Ltd and GSB Prospection Ltd)

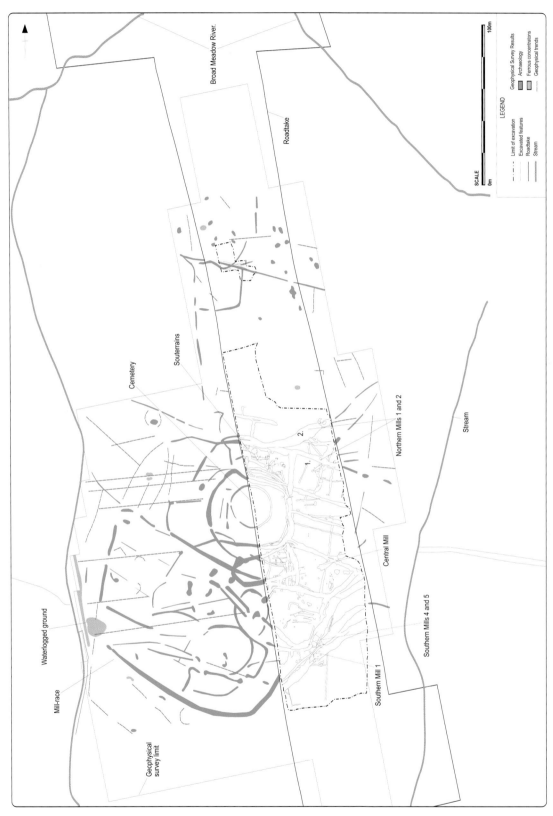

Illus. 3—Plan of Raystown showing geophysical survey data and excavated remains (CRDS Ltd and GSB Prospection Ltd)

later agriculture had disturbed at least a further 40 burials, which were indicated by disarticulated bone scattered through the soil. Sometimes this was placed in clusters known as charnel deposits, in which bones disturbed during grave-digging were stacked, either in the grave or in a separate pit. Radiocarbon dates obtained from the human bone indicate burial between the early fifth and the late 10th century (for details see Appendix 1). The burials were in simple, shallow and mostly unlined graves, and the skeletons were generally aligned with heads to the west. The tightly bound postures of a number of skeletons suggested that these people had been buried in shrouds. Others may have been dressed differently for burial: objects such as an iron knife and an iron pin (probably ringed) may indicate this. Other objects found included a copper-alloy ring and, perhaps most poignantly, a blue glass bead at the neck of a child. The practice of including personal objects, jewellery and dress-fasteners is seen in other, contemporaneous burials in Britain and Ireland (O'Brien 1999, 179–84).

The human bone was analysed by osteoarchaeologist Linda Fibiger. The burials comprised 68 adults, three adolescents, 20 juveniles and two older infants. During this period children frequently did not live beyond four years of age. The percentage of juveniles and infants is very low, and neonatal babies (babies from birth to four weeks) are absent from the Raystown burials, suggesting that they may have been buried elsewhere. The majority of children at Raystown who had died at between one and eight years of age were buried in a specific area to the south of an inner ring-ditch. Of the adults at Raystown, 70 per cent had lived beyond 36–45 years, and women had lived longer than men. Measurements of stature showed that women were taller than those on comparable early medieval Irish sites, perhaps owing to diet and/or hereditary factors. Chemical analysis of isotopes laid down in bone during life indicated that the diet at Raystown was mainly land-based.

Disease was a factor of everyday life, and relatively high numbers of adults suffered from systemic infections such as tuberculosis. These would have been more prevalent than the skeletal remains suggest, as only severe cases leave impacts on bone. The close proximity of large numbers of animals would have contributed to the spread of disease. Lifestyle and work also directly affected human bone. This could be observed in patterns of degenerative joint disease in men, with compression of the lower spine indicating heavy lifting, while women had degenerative changes of the neck, suggesting repetitive back-and-forth movement. Women generally suffered more than men from non-spinal joint disease. The exception to this pattern was that men had higher levels of joint disease in the wrist and shoulder on their less dominant side. The archaeological evidence suggests many activities that could have caused these patterns in women and men, including hauling timbers and stones, digging for mill-races, reaping, threshing, food preparation and tending large numbers of animals.

A number of burials demonstrate the violent nature of early medieval Irish life. Two male burials had cuts to the bone, indicating blade trauma. One had been struck on the neck and jaw, and the other had more than 108 cut-marks all over his body. Although this translates into a smaller number of injuries, as each wound could leave multiple impacts, it suggests a ferocious attack indicative of armed combat.

Unusual burial practice was also in evidence. A male burial was inserted in a former drying kiln, a considerable distance from the other burials. Unlike the other burials he was covered with stones and laid in a north-south position on his right side with legs flexed.

Souterrains

Northern Mill 2
Headrace

Northern Mill 2
Undercroft

Northern Mill 1
Headrace

Northern Mill 1
Undercroft

Pennanular Enclosure

Outer Burial Enclosure

Northern Habitation Area

Subrectangular Enclosure

Kilns

Illus. 4—Aerial photograph of the north-eastern part of the Raystown site (CRDS Ltd and Studio Lab)

Illus. 5—Unusual burial in the remains of a kiln on the edge of the enclosure. This man was buried a considerable distance from the other burials and was laid in a north–south position (CRDS Ltd)

The outer burial enclosure later cut through this burial (Illus. 5). Why was he deliberately placed away from the other burials and treated differently?

Living

On either side of the cemetery were dense areas of settlement. To the north was an area paved with small stones. It was littered with animal bone and artefacts such as bone and iron pins, needles, iron tools and a horse bit. Gullies and post-holes suggested a structure, possibly a house, and a small stone-built cereal-drying kiln. Two souterrains were uncovered in this area (Illus. 6). The first had a narrow, low, winding passageway leading to a rounded chamber. It was initially timber-built, with the entrance having been replaced in stone. Wooden souterrains are relatively unusual in County Meath. The second souterrain was stone-built and had a corbelled roof. It had a narrow passageway leading to a large, rectangular chamber. This structure had a rear exit through a lintelled opening (Illus. 7). It is not known which souterrain was built first, and scientific dating is currently under way.

It is clear that the souterrains were later additions to the settlement. This area of Brega was originally thought to have had relatively few souterrains (Clinton 2001, 38), but excavations are now suggesting a complex picture. The northern settlement area and the cemetery were later enclosed by a large, subrectangular enclosure (Illus. 4), indicating that the people felt the need to distinguish this area of the site from the farming activity outside. To the south of the cemetery was a dense pattern of gullies, hearths and a probable house site.

Illus. 6—Excavation in progress of two souterrains in the northern area of the Raystown site (Hawkeye)

Illus. 7—Souterrain in northern area with rear exit through lintelled opening, with inset of excavation in progress (CRDS Ltd)

After the harvest—grain and grinding

Features relating to work and production, with field enclosures, possible livestock enclosures, kilns and mills, dominated the land outside the cemetery and settlement areas. Ditches radiating out from the core enclosures subdivided it. These ditches ran downslope and would have formed drains and boundaries. Several of them had been recut numerous times over the centuries. Repeated actions such as recutting boundaries suggest that the inhabitants strictly maintained and controlled the way that land was divided.

Five cereal-drying kilns were found in these outlying areas. They were all figure-of-eight-shaped pits. These structures, found on early medieval sites throughout Ireland, allowed heat to dry cereal crops gently after harvesting and threshing. The surviving pits are the remains of a more complex kiln structure that would have had a clay or wattle superstructure. Processing of the soil from the kilns recovered large quantities of barley, oats, wheat, rye and weed species that had been accidentally charred during drying. The drying was essential in the damp and cold Irish climate. It staved off decay and allowed the grain to be milled more efficiently.

The remains of up to eight watermills were excavated at Raystown, along with the substantial watercourses that fed them. They were concentrated in clusters: two in the northern part of the site, one in the centre and up to five in the southern area. Watermills had been introduced to Ireland by the mid-first millennium AD, possibly from mainland Europe (Rynne 2000, 47). They are known from both archaeological and historical evidence. Watermills revolutionised the processing of cereals, which had previously been ground by hand on quern-stones.

At Raystown the water source was situated a considerable distance to the south of the excavated areas and is likely to have been a natural or artificial channel connecting to the Broad Meadow River. The levels of the mill-races were carefully designed to bring water from the source to the mills. This meant that some of the races had to be cut to a depth of over 2 m into the hillside. The water may have provided a resource for other purposes, such as watering animals, washing and drinking. The mill-races led to the mill, in some cases via a reservoir or a pond, and the water was held in place by an earthen, wooden or stone dam.

The remains of the mills themselves consisted of the undercrofts or wheel-pits (Illus. 8 & 9). The majority used horizontal wheels and were fed water from the race or pond by a wooden chute known as a flume. This allowed water to be directed at force at the wheel, which in turn drove a shaft that turned the millstones in the upper building. This building was supported on wooden and/or stone foundations that survived in the waterlogged conditions in five of the mill sites. The mill buildings were variously supported by large oak base plates, which had carpentry joints to hold upright timbers, by large posts driven into the undercrofts or by stone walls bonded with clay (Illus. 10). Horizontal mills of these types can still be seen operating in parts of the world such as Bosnia, Spain and Portugal and were in common use in Ireland until the 20th century (Moog 1994; Knox 1907).

A vertical undershot mill may also have been present in the southern area of the site. In this type of mill, water runs through a race and enters the mill at the same level as the base of the vertical wheel. This required a gearing system to drive the shaft and millstones. No millstones or wheels were recovered, and it is likely that these were intentionally removed from each structure because of their high value. The mills were radiocarbon-dated to between the seventh and the 10th century AD. (Dendrochronology or tree-ring dating could not be employed because the oak used in the construction of the mills came from

Illus. 8—Aerial photograph of mills under excavation (Hawkeye)

fast-growing, slightly warped trees that did not have enough rings.) Owing to the symmetrical arrangement of mill-races on either side of the site, it is possible that pairs of mills were used together. The people of the site were physically and socially defined by them.

Animals

While the physical remains of the mills are spectacular, animal husbandry clearly played a large part in the lives and subsistence of the inhabitants of this site. More than 700 kg of animal bone was recovered during excavations, and a corral-like feature was noted in the results of the geophysical survey to the west of the site. Analysis of this bone is continuing, but it is clear that cattle, pig, sheep/goat, horse, deer and bird are all represented. Examination of this bone will aim to discover whether differences in the patterns of animal use over the centuries can be distinguished.

End of a settlement

The current dating and artefactual evidence suggests that the mills, settlement and cemetery had been abandoned by the 12th century. The latest of the mill structures contained a sherd of medieval pottery in the soil that filled the upper part of it. Anglo-Norman settlers arrived

Illus. 9—Northern Mill 2 under excavation (CRDS Ltd)

in the area in the late 12th century, and the first mention of the name Raystown is in a 14th-century document, which refers to Walter Ray, a free tenant, with land in Raystown (Orpen 1921, 73). The original name of the townland is unknown, and there are no early medieval references that can be linked to the site. Plough-pebbles, which are small stones for protecting the sides of wooden ploughs, were found during the excavation and suggest that the land continued to be cultivated in the 13th century. The recovery of a small number of medieval potsherds and an iron candleholder suggest continued occupation nearby.

Towards meaning

Raystown clearly has a fascinating tale to tell and raises a number of important issues. The earliest dated activity is the burial of the dead. Cemeteries form powerful symbolic places in the landscape and signify spiritual claims to the land. Burials began in Raystown at approximately the time when the first Irish Christians sought a bishop from Rome. Burials of a relatively small community continued into the 10th century. There are considerable difficulties in distinguishing Christian from non-Christian ancestral cemeteries. There is also confusion about how ancestral cemeteries were allowed to continue. Circular burial enclosures around burial sites had a long ancestry in Ireland and were used to surround

Illus. 10—Reconstruction of Northern Mill 2 (Simon Dick for CRDS Ltd)

groups of inhumations (burials of articulated skeletons) in the early centuries AD. Some of these may have been focused on a central or principal burial. Circular enclosures were also used to surround monastic sites, often including outer settlements. In this sense Raystown is different—only the cemetery was enclosed in the initial phase.

Excavations at Raystown have allowed a close examination of the context of milling in early medieval Ireland. The Raystown community lived through the building, maintenance and use of mills. Mills have often been recovered in small-scale excavations but can rarely be placed in context with their surroundings. In recent years a strong link has emerged between church sites and large-scale milling. Monastic and ecclesiastical sites such as Nendrum, Co. Down, and, on a smaller scale, Killoteran, Co. Waterford, (Murphy & Rathbone, this volume) used watermills to process cereals. In these cases the mills were situated at some distance from the monastery. Documentary evidence suggests that farmers, such as those who inhabited ringforts, and religious sites had access to, or a share in, mill

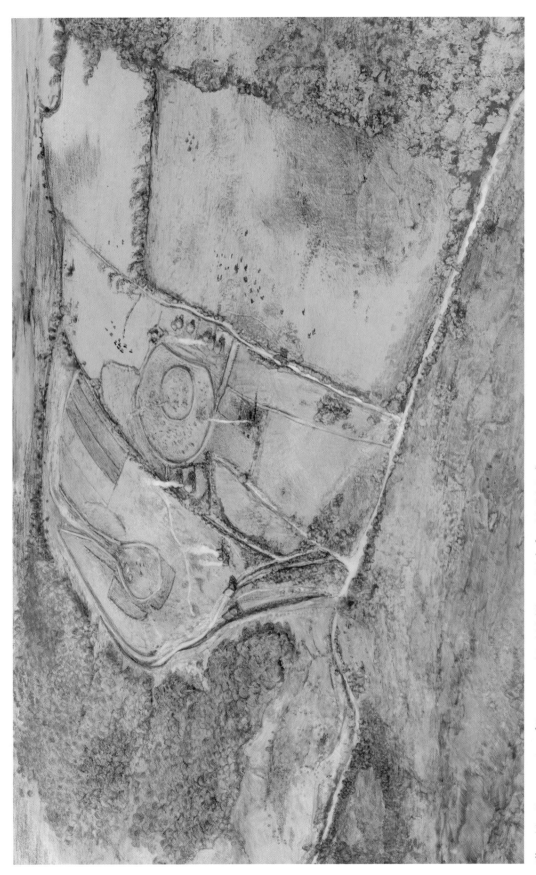

Illus. 11—Reconstruction of Raystown c. AD 900 (Simon Dick for CRDS Ltd)

sites. The mills were central to life at Raystown and suggest that the people needed to maximise the potential of the location through the power of water, even if it meant engineering complex and labour-intensive watercourses, probably with specialist assistance. Millwrights are well attested in early medieval documents and held the same kind of status as shipbuilders. All of this suggests planning, control and power.

How does Raystown differ from traditional church sites, which may also have contained a cemetery, settlement, farm and mills? A number of sites have emerged in recent years that include cemeteries, large enclosures and, in some cases, souterrains and mills. None have unambiguous church buildings or associations. These sites have a different range of activities from those at ringforts and are generally of a much larger scale. Indeed their scale suggests that they may have been controlled by larger interests, possibly a significant ecclesiastical site, such as Dunshaughlin, or by local rulers, such as the kings at Lagore crannóg, in the case of Raystown.

Conclusion

The discovery of Raystown on the N2 Finglas–Ashbourne road scheme is a dramatic illustration of how archaeological research can flow from previously unknown sites. Research-based archaeology picks its subject carefully, moving from the general to the particular. The building of roads and the associated archaeological investigations have meant that unknown sites and new site types have emerged. With scientific excavation and analysis these sites can change and initiate research agendas. The site at Raystown tells a fascinating story of a people's efforts to produce food through technology. Moreover, the evidence from this site can be used to discuss power relationships between people, both on the site and within the region. Although the mills are silent, the intentions of those who built them will occupy the thoughts of anyone with an interest in early medieval Ireland for some time to come.

Acknowledgements

Sincere thanks to the excavation team, especially to the supervisors, Stephanie Durning, Kevin Martin, Mairéad McLaughlin, Alex Southeran, Mandy Stephens and Bernice Watts, to the post-excavation team, particularly Madeleine Murray, post-excavation manager, and to Niall Lynch and the drafting team. The excavation would not have been possible without the management and advice of Finola O'Carroll, project manager for CRDS Ltd. I would like to express my gratitude to Dr Maria FitzGerald, project archaeologist for Meath County Council. Thanks to Simon Dick for the site reconstruction drawings and to all of the specialists who have contributed. Thanks to Colin Rynne, Department of Archaeology, University College Cork, for comment on milling technology. All errors and omissions are my own.

9. Excavation of a children's burial ground at Tonybaun, Ballina, County Mayo

Joanna Nolan

Illus. 1—Excavation of an infant skeleton at Tonybaun, Co. Mayo (courtesy of Chris Randolph)

In 2003, Mayo County Council archaeologists undertook the excavation of five archaeological areas in advance of the construction of the N26 Ballina to Bohola (Stage 1) road scheme. These excavations were conducted on behalf of the National Roads Authority and Mayo County Council and included the excavation of a known children's burial ground or *cillín* in Tonybaun townland, 6 km south of Ballina (Illus. 1 & 2). It is recorded in the Record of Monuments and Places as MA039-107 (NGR 124790, 312310; height 20 m OD; excavation licence no. 03E0139). Some 248 burials were discovered at the site; subsequent radiocarbon dating indicates a period of use beginning in the late 15th century and ending in the mid-20th century. The majority of those interred here were infants. Archaeological investigation of this type of site can be a difficult experience, especially, in this case, for the local community, who had a strong attachment to this burial ground. The excavation led to the reburial of these individuals in the parish graveyard at Ballynahaglish with full funeral rites. These individuals, who had been set apart in the past, were ultimately reintegrated into the wider community.

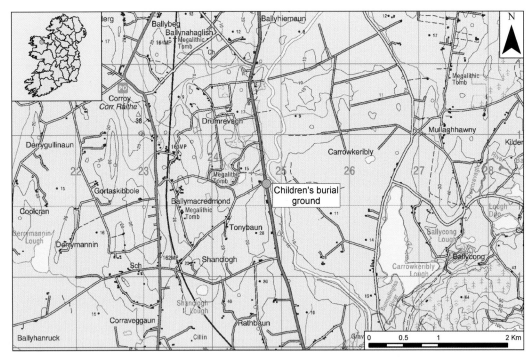

Illus. 2—Location map of children's burial ground at Tonybaun, Co. Mayo (based on the Ordnance Survey Ireland map)

Separate burial

Children's burial grounds are fairly common sites in Ireland. They were used for the interment of those who, for various reasons, were considered ineligible for burial in consecrated ground. This practice may have come about as a result of canon law in the 1600s, which stated that such people were to be laid in a place set apart. But it probably also has roots in the traditions of the early church. There are the well-attested examples of the separate burial of men and women at ecclesiastical sites such as Inishmurray, Co. Sligo, Clonmacnois, Co. Offaly, and Iona, Scotland. There was also a tradition of the burial of men who had died in battle in the least-favoured areas of a graveyard, usually north of the church (Hamlin & Foley 1983).

Those buried during the modern phases of children's burial grounds were generally stillborns and babies who died at birth and had not been baptised. Several other classes of people were seen as similarly ineligible for burial in consecrated ground (see Channing & Randolph-Quinney, this volume). Suicide victims were considered excommunicate, as were those who were perceived to have died unrepentant, such as strangers, criminals, men who had died in battle, the mentally retarded and famine victims. Mothers who had died in childbirth and had not been 'churched' (i.e. had not undergone a prayer ceremony after childbirth) and older children, perhaps because they were not considered as full members of the community, were also sometimes interred in these burial grounds (Leigh Fry 1999, 176–87; Donnelly et al. 1995; Hamlin & Foley 1983). This practice did not fully end in Ireland until the 1960s, after the Second Vatican Council.

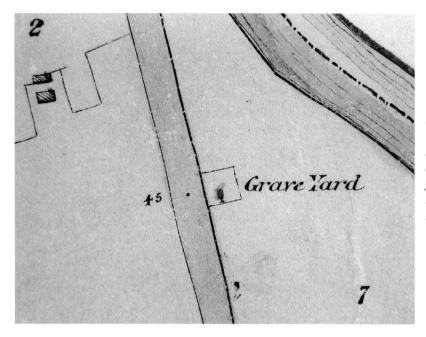

Illus. 3—Extract from 1840 estate map showing Tonybaun children's burial ground (courtesy of Alan Moloney, Mount Falcon)

These burial grounds tended to develop on the sites of earlier, often ecclesiastical, monuments. The relatives of the deceased were probably selecting locations that appeared to have sacred associations. Other monuments reused for this purpose in the west of Ireland include ringforts and prehistoric burial mounds. Such sites would have had religious and/or superstitious associations (Crombie 1988; Aldridge 1969).

The Tonybaun *cillín*

The burial ground at Tonybaun was located beside the original N26 in the corner of a large field on the bank of the River Moy. It was roughly rectangular in outline (17 m north–south by 22 m) and was raised above the surrounding field by about 1 m. It was heavily overgrown by briars, bushes and four or five large sycamore trees. During the Moy drainage scheme in the 1960s, material dredged from the river was deposited and spread over the fields around the site. Local information indicates that the surrounding fields were used for the commercial growing of potatoes up until the early 1900s. The burial ground was well known in the area and there was strong local attachment to it. The last burial appears to have taken place here about 50 years ago.

Because these burial grounds are often sited on earlier monuments, there was a possibility that the vicinity of the site could contain further features relating to earlier uses. A geophysical survey was carried out around the site to investigate this possibility. This survey was carried out by GeoArc Ltd in December 2002 around all but the west side of the site (where the N26 abutted it), and extended out for a distance of 30–40 m. It identified a very subtle anomaly curving around the eastern half of the site, suggesting a large curvilinear enclosure beyond the edge of the roadtake. The excavated area was extended to the north and south of the *cillín* to test for the presence of a ditch. These cuttings revealed that the anomaly had been caused by stone and gravel dredged from the River Moy in the 1960s, which had been buried here to level these fields.

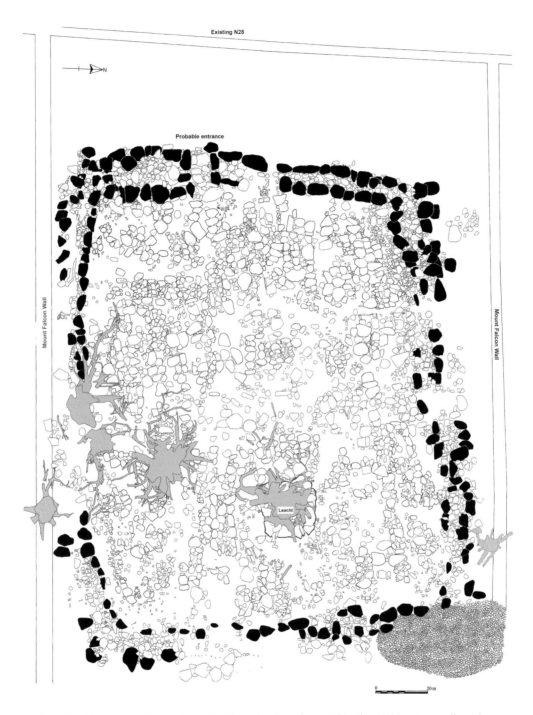

Illus. 4—Plan of burial ground showing the earlier boundary within the 19th-century walls and concentration of stones forming rectangular settings or grave-markers (Mayo County Council)

At the time of the excavation the site was enclosed by stone walls built of quarried, roughly squared limestone on all but the east side. These are similar to the walls enclosing the nearby Mount Falcon demesne and it is likely that they were built by the owners of this estate. The Name Book of the first Ordnance Survey (OS) records construction at Mount Falcon in 1826, and an estate map from 1840 based on the first edition OS six-inch map depicts these walls (Illus. 3). This would date the construction of the walls to just before the Famine (1845–48). Along each side of the burial ground, set 1–2 m inside these 'Mount Falcon' walls and on a slightly different axis, were remnants of what appeared to be an earlier site boundary (Illus. 4). This consisted of linear, contiguous settings of rounded, mainly granite boulders set upright. Excavation revealed that this boundary was constructed using drystone walling techniques, whereby large basal stones were set on/in the ground in two parallel rows to form the base. The stones that survived appear to be the foundation courses, but these presumably supported upper courses built with smaller stones, which did not survive. The later walls extended the burial area to the north and west and it is likely, therefore, that at least some of the skeletons buried between the two walls date from the Famine.

Grave-markers within the burial ground were mostly masked by vegetation and leaf litter, but some protruded very slightly above ground. It was possible to discern that a number of markers consisted of a few stones in roughly rectangular settings. Two layers of topsoil covered the burial ground. The upper one was probably generated by the overgrowth and leaf litter that had built up since the site ceased to be used. It contained a good deal of modern rubbish and had nearly covered the grave-markers completely. When this upper layer was removed these settings turned out to be more complex than the initial survey had indicated. They were found to be roughly rectangular and made up of generally uniform-sized stones. The best examples were quite regular. The north and south sides were delimited by rough parallel rows of stones. The enclosed area was filled with smaller, 'filler' stones, often set on edge but sometimes laid flat or simply jammed in against one another. The head (west) and foot (east) ends were sometimes marked by large stones laid flat. Locally available granites and sandstones were used to build these settings. Not all the grave settings conformed to this pattern. Others were comprised of spreads of small stones set rather haphazardly in a loosely rectangular shape.

One hundred stone settings were recorded but only 25 of them closely corresponded with underlying burials. The others sometimes partly overlay burials or covered burials that had decayed away completely. Also, some of the graves underlying these settings had disturbed earlier burials so that partial skeletons were found around the edges of the settings. The settings seem to have been constructed on and within the lower layer of topsoil. The modern, mainly children's, burials were nearly all contained within this layer (Illus. 5).

A second layer of burials underlay the modern graves (Illus. 6). These rested at the base of the lower topsoil and within the underlying boulder clay. They have been interpreted as representing the earliest phases of the site; they had no associated modern material, such as coffin nails or timbers, and no infants were present in this level. This lower layer of graves appears to contain two types of burial: those aligned ESE–WNW and those aligned east–west (the head laid westwards in both cases). Most of the skeletons that were buried in the former alignment were female, while the east–west-aligned skeletons were predominantly male. It may be that these distinct alignments represent some form of differentiation, if not separation, between the two genders, perhaps originating in the medieval practice of separate burials for men and women. Unfortunately, the range of the radiocarbon dates (AD 1475-1638 to 1664-1951, see Appendix 1 for details) is too broad to do more than suggest that the male burials could be slightly earlier than the females and that there is no definite chronological separation between the two groups.

Illus. 5—Plan of upper layer of burials containing the modern, mainly children's, burials (Mayo County Council)

Excavation of the burials

Once recorded, the marker settings were removed; the area delimited by them was taken as the extent of the grave they marked and excavated as such. It was found that these settings had been placed on top of the graves after they had been backfilled, so that revealing the actual burials was sometimes problematic. Because graves had been dug into the lower layer of topsoil and backfilled with the same topsoil, there was no obvious cut. Occasionally, the grave fill was looser than the surrounding topsoil and this was the only indication of a grave-cut.

Illus. 6—Plan of lower layer of burials, which provided the samples for radiocarbon dating (Mayo County Council)

Many of the burials were found to have been interred in wooden coffins held together by iron nails. These were typically 0.7 m long and 0.2 m wide at the head (west), tapering to 0.15 m at the feet (east). Samples from five coffins were identified as Scots pine by Ellen OCarroll of the Archaeology Company. In a few examples enough of the wood survived to give an indication of the structure of these coffins. The grain of surviving wood fragments indicated that the bases were formed of short planks laid transversely; the lid boards appeared to run longitudinally. The presence of coffin nails in the chest, midriff or knee areas of their related skeletons was common. This suggested that the lid boards might have been held together by nails and wooden cross-pieces, or cleats. The coffin sides appeared to have been single planks set on edge. The nails were sometimes recovered in two layers and often indicated the outline of the coffin from which they derived. Because there were few obvious grave-cuts (and sometimes no surviving bone), the burials were often located solely by revealing the coffin nails that surrounded them.

Bone preservation on this site was often poor; in many cases only fragments of skull and decayed crumbs of the rest of the skeleton survived. The soil pH was tested by the local Teagasc office and was found to be quite low (5.5–7), contributing to the decay of these fragile bones. Where the decay was extreme, the soil containing the fragments within the coffin outline was bagged for reburial. There had also been a good deal of site disturbance, which also hampered bone recovery. Tree roots and animal burrows were common, and caused damage to the graves. Stone settings and skeletons had often been broken up and redeposited as a result.

Analysis of the skeletal remains

The excavation team were advised on the handling, recording and storage of the skeletons by Linda Lynch, osteoarchaeologist with Aegis Archaeology Ltd. Subsequent analysis of the remains was carried out by Dr Eileen Murphy, Queen's University, Belfast; her conclusions are given below. Nine skeletons were sampled for radiocarbon dating at Oxford University Radiocarbon Accelerator Unit. They were chosen from the stratigraphically lowest layer of graves (Illus. 6) so that the date of the earliest use of the site could be ascertained. Two of the samples failed to date because the bone was too decayed to produce any collagen—the protein usually extracted for radiocarbon dating. The other seven produced wide-ranging dates from AD 1475–1638 to AD 1664–1951 (see Appendix 1). It is likely that the site has been in continuous use as a burial ground since the late 15th/early 16th century.

A total of 248 skeletons were recovered from the site—181 children and 67 adults. Of these, 237 were sufficiently complete for analysis and could be allocated to the following age ranges:

- 147 infants (up to two years)
- 23 children (two to six years)
- 4 juveniles (six to 12 years)
- 8 adolescents (12 to 17 years)
- 55 adults: 18 female, 15 male, 22 indeterminate

As expected, the majority of burials were of infants. However, the presence of all other age groups in this burial ground reflects the practice of considering a broad range of individuals as excommunicate, or not in a state of repentance, and therefore candidates for burial in unconsecrated ground.

The poor preservation of the bones made full analysis difficult but it was possible, nonetheless, to identify several characteristics of this population. The most prevalent adult age at death for both sexes was in the 25–35 years age bracket; males who survived beyond this age seemed more likely to live into older adulthood (i.e. >45 years). Women were more susceptible to earlier death, possibly owing to the danger of death during pregnancy. The infants were notably small at birth, perhaps as a result of poor maternal health during pregnancy.

The surviving teeth presented a picture of poor oral hygiene, evidenced by several dental problems such as cavities, periodontal or gum disease and tooth loss. This was more prevalent among the females. The diet of these people may have contributed to their dental problems. They may have been eating starchy tubers or cereal grains in soft, sticky, porridge-like forms, which contained sugar–starch combinations that caused tooth decay. Soil samples taken from the stomach regions of some of the burials were examined by Dr Meriel McClatchie at University College Cork. Cereal remains were identified in two of these samples, which initially seemed to confirm a link between diet and dental health; the findings were inconclusive, however, as cereal grains were also recovered from non-burial contexts.

The adults' teeth gave further indications of the health of this population through a condition called dental enamel hypoplasia. This is a linear pitting or grooving on the tooth enamel and is caused by conditions like fever, starvation, congenital infections, low birth weight and parasitic infestation, all of which may occur while the teeth are growing. Thirty-three skeletons were suitable for enamel examination. Most of the incidents that caused the hypoplasia occurred between the ages of two and four and a half. Grooves on the teeth of one of the females who had died at a young age (17–25 years) revealed three separate episodes of ill-health, which may have contributed to her early death. Other information revealed by osteological analysis includes the rare discovery that one of the females (25–35 years of age) was a pipe-smoker, as wear patterns on her front teeth indicated 'pipe-smoker's clench'.

Another female (25–35 years) was found to have been pregnant when she died: fragmentary remains in her pelvic region were identified as the bones of an infant or late foetus. Three blade injuries were identified on the skull of this woman and it would appear that she had been murdered. This would have made her doubly ineligible for burial in consecrated ground—both as a murder victim and because she could not have been 'churched' prior to her death.

Funerary practices

Several of the infants were buried with one or more shroud pins: a total of 53 were recovered from 27 graves. These were made of copper wire, with heads of twisted wire wrapped around the blunt end. Where they were found in direct association with the skeleton they tended to be on the brow area or at the neck, probably where the shrouds were fastened. Other items discovered in direct association with skeletons were buttons, a pair of spectacles, wool and fabric, a small crucifix and a small plastic picture-frame of a type commonly used for religious pictures in the recent past. Although this site type has been associated with secretive, unceremonious and rapid disposal of the dead, some of these grave-goods suggest that care and some religious observances were associated with these burials.

Further evidence for some form of spiritual or commemorative activities is provided by the presence on the site of an altar-like structure (Illus. 7). This has been classified as a *leacht*,

Illus. 7—The leacht *or altar cairn after removal of a tree stump* (Mayo County Council)

or outdoor altar cairn. These structures occur in many early medieval burial grounds and have been dated to as early as the late first millennium AD. They may have been used at various times as reliquary shrines, pilgrimage stations, altars and burial-markers (White Marshall & Rourke 2000, 29; O'Dowd 1998). This particular example is stratigraphically earlier than the modern burial layer but may have continued in use throughout the life of the burial ground, as has been seen at ecclesiastical sites like Inishmurray, Co. Sligo (O'Sullivan & Ó Carragáin, in press). No evidence of a burial was found associated with this *leacht*. The presence of over 700 small, water-rolled stones, mainly quartz or quartzite, scattered in the ground surrounding and within the *leacht* suggests that its purpose was ritual or memorial. These stones were very rounded pebbles that had obviously been chosen for their 'eye-catching' qualities. There is no natural source for these stones in the immediate vicinity of the site. They may have been brought by mourners and left on the *leacht* as part of a ritual round, or *turas,* accompanying prayers for the dead.

Evidence of earlier occupation

Traces of prehistoric and early medieval activity were also discovered at Tonybaun. Worked chert and flint were common, both in the burial ground and in the test trenches around it. A total of 247 struck pieces of flint and chert were found, consisting of blades, flakes, scrapers, cores, a hollow-based arrowhead, two stone axeheads and a microlith. These artefacts represent very early prehistoric activity around the site from the Early Mesolithic

Illus. 8—Stone-lined, Iron Age furnace pit located to the north of the burial ground (Mayo County Council)

period onwards, but subsequent reuse of the land has completely mixed this material into the topsoil so that their original contexts are lost.

About 40 m north of the burial ground three groups of features indicating metalworking activities, such as ore extraction and smelting, were found. These consisted of furnace pits, containing charcoal-rich fills densely mixed with furnace slag, dug into the sandy natural clay. There were spreads of what appeared to be dumped material around two of the pits, and one of these spreads contained flux-lining slags (formed when the clay edges of the pit became vitrified by heat during the firing process). The most complex of the three furnace pits was stone-lined and had a small slab laid flat to form the base (Illus. 8). This pit has been radiocarbon-dated to 477–210 BC (UB-6765; see Appendix 1 for details). A second furnace pit was radiocarbon-dated to 166 BC–AD 25 (UB-6763; see Appendix 1), dating this metalworkng activity to the Iron Age.

On the periphery of the site the test trenches revealed a series of cultivation ridge and furrows that were of significantly different character to lazy beds encountered in the wider area around the site. The cultivation ridges, which appear to have been hand-dug, were small in comparison to the lazy beds. They were rather 'lumpy' in profile and were not perfectly parallel. The ridges were encountered outside the edge of the burial ground at the north-west corner and outside part of the eastern edge. In both cases they had been truncated by both the burial ground and by lazy beds. A few faint traces of them also survived in a small area underlying burials in the south-east section of the burial ground. Charcoal from the furrows at the north-west corner has been radiocarbon-dated to AD 467–648 (UB-6764; see Appendix 1).

Agricultural activity during the early medieval period is further indicated by twenty rotary quern-stone fragments found in the burial ground, eight of which were reused as parts of stone settings and in the *leacht*. In addition, several scatters of furnace slag were recorded in the burial ground and a fragment of a metalworker's small clay crucible was found incorporated into one of the stone settings. A charcoal-flecked sandy horizon containing lumps of vitrified sand and iron slag was found underlying and cut by the burials

Illus. 9—Reburial plot in Ballynahaglish cemetery, Knockmore, Ballina (Mayo County Council)

in the south-west corner of the site. It was interpreted as residue from metalworking and has been radiocarbon-dated to AD 882–1015 (UB-6767; see Appendix 1). This was underlain by a further activity layer distinguishable by its charcoal-rich content; it has been radiocarbon-dated to AD 772–969 (UB-6766; see Appendix 1). Unfortunately, this layer produced no finds that would assist in its further interpretation.

Although there is good evidence, in the form of both dates and artefacts, for several periods of activity on this site and within its immediate vicinity, the recent reuse of this location as a burial ground and the modern cultivation in its environs have destroyed many of the early features that presumably existed here. One of the main questions with a burial ground of this type is whether it represents the latest incarnation of an early medieval, possibly ecclesiastical, site. There are certainly tantalising traces of early medieval activity here. The narrow plough ridges, the quern-stone fragments, a dated layer of metalworking residue and the crucible fragment suggest that this site was used for agricultural and metalworking activities during the early medieval period. Attempts to date the burials firmly have not been very successful, as the date ranges produced are generally too broad to be truly meaningful (see Appendix 1). Nonetheless, the radiocarbon dating has established that none of the burials pre-date the 15th century.

Conclusion

On 19 June 2005, with the agreement of the National Museum of Ireland, the skeletons were reburied in the local Ballynahaglish cemetery, Knockmore, after a funeral service in the parish church by Dr John Fleming, Bishop of Killala, and Bishop Richard Henderson, Church of Ireland Bishop of Tuam, Killala and Achonry. There was a large attendance from the local community and it appeared that their understandable reservations about the removal of the burial ground were largely addressed by this ceremony and reburial. A memorial plaque giving details of the burials and the excavation has been erected by Mayo County Council in the graveyard (Illus. 9). Another plaque was erected on the site of the burial ground to mark its original location.

The burials excavated at Tonybaun represent all ages of the community from which they derived but there was a preponderance of infant graves. The skeletal analysis indicates a population existing in poor conditions; children would have been particularly susceptible to the exigencies of poverty and famine. It is likely that many of these babies did not survive birth. Excavating the graves of so many children was a sad experience, but the most poignant graves were those of three sets of twins. All were interred together, and in one case it appeared that the babies had been arranged in such a way that one had his/her arms around the other. This excavation gave us a glimpse of a time in Ireland when infant mortality, though high, was not acknowledged. The aspect of exclusion associated with this site type makes these infant burials especially tragic. The reburial at least gave us and the surrounding parish the opportunity to commemorate these lost lives and to give them at last an acknowledged place in the community.

Acknowledgements

I would like to thank Paul Clarke for assistance with all aspects of this project, Margaret McNamara for research assistance, David Loftus for the line drawings, Jerry O'Sullivan and Tomás Ó Carragáin for their pre-publication typescript of their book on Inishmurray, and Alan Moloney of Mount Falcon for the photograph of his estate map. I would also like to thank Fr Harrison and the people of Knockmore parish for all the help and information they shared with us, all the excavation team and members of staff at the Regional Design Office, Mayo County Council, especially Pat Staunton, project engineer, Tony McNulty, senior engineer, and Gerry Walsh, project archaeologist.

10. Archaeological aerial survey—a bird's-eye view of the M7/M8 in County Laois

Lisa Courtney

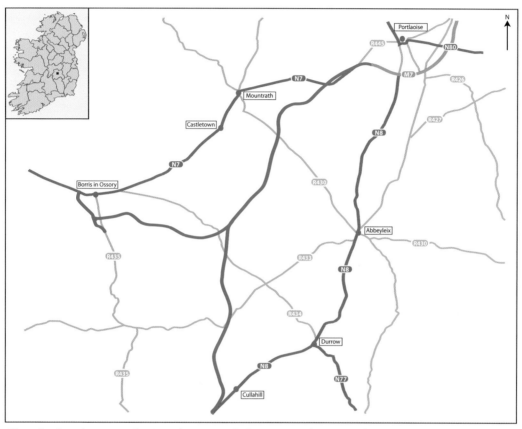

Illus. 1—Location map showing the route of the M7 Portlaoise–Castletown/M8 Portlaoise–Cullahill Motorway scheme, indicated in red (Kildare County Council National Roads Design Office)

The M7 Portlaoise–Castletown/M8 Portlaoise–Cullahill Motorway scheme through County Laois will comprise 41 km of motorway and 11 km of link roads (Illus. 1). It will commence from the existing Portlaoise Bypass and tie in with the N7 Castletown–Nenagh road scheme, south of Borris in Ossory, and the M8 Cullahill–Cashel Motorway scheme, south of Cullahill. The M7/M8 scheme is the largest infrastructural project to be undertaken in County Laois. The proposed motorway is routed through a rural landscape, with the existing land use being almost exclusively agricultural. Villages and settlements in the environs of the motorway include Borris in Ossory, Cullahill, Ballycolla, Aghaboe and Clogh. The landscape is characterised by well-drained, gently undulating, broad valleys, giving rise to good-quality pastureland and pockets of bogland. Remnants of historical landscapes and woodland demesne planting occur along the route at Abbeyleix, Castledurrow, Donore, Palmerhill, Lismore and Granston.

Illus. 2—Ringfort (RMP No. LA034-034) in Oldtown townland in the vicinity of the southernmost section of the M8 Portlaoise–Cullahill Motorway Scheme. Although not directly affected by the scheme, this site was photographed as part of the route selection phase (Margaret Gowen & Co. Ltd)

Archaeological aerial survey

The preferred route assessed in the Environmental Impact Statement (EIS) was selected after a detailed route selection process that considered, among other things, the potential impact of the proposed routes on the archaeological heritage. The archaeological study in the EIS was based on desk study, field inspection, and aerial and geophysical surveys. The use of aerial survey at the earliest stage of road design, in conjunction with other techniques such as field inspection and documentary research, assists in the assessment of the archaeological potential of a road scheme and informs the later testing and excavation phases.

Owing to the outbreak of foot-and-mouth disease, an aerial inspection was undertaken in August 2001 at the route selection stage of the project. A further survey was conducted in February 2002 for the archaeological impact statement report. This low-level survey (500–1000 ft), with the use of oblique photography, was carried out to identify and determine the extent of previously known and unknown archaeological features and to examine areas of known archaeological potential.

The low-flying survey comprised a direct visual examination of the ground from the air by a qualified archaeologist using digital photography and 35 mm and 60 mm colour print

Illus. 3—Gortnaclea Castle (RMP No. LA023-016) with surrounding bawn (enclosing feature) from the east, August 2001 (Margaret Gowen & Co. Ltd)

photography. The photographs were taken at an oblique angle to maximise the recognition of subtle features. Given the known level of intensive agricultural practices along the scheme, aerial survey was a particularly important tool for identifying levelled or partly levelled sites that had no visible expression at ground level. It also provided an excellent opportunity to view the proposed road scheme from a different perspective and ensured a familiarity with the landscape.

To realise the full benefit of an aerial survey it is imperative that documentary work is carried out before the flight so that the location of recorded monuments and current land use and type can be assessed and any limitations (for example, vegetation cover or underlying geology) in identifying features are known in advance. Certain types of monuments are easier to identity from the air. As this can create a bias in the record, it is useful to identify the location of recorded monuments in advance, so that the features are known before the flight.

The success of an archaeological aerial survey is also dependent on the weather and recent weather patterns. For example, the ideal conditions to photograph subtle earthworks or relic field systems are when the sun is low in the sky, in either winter or late evening in summer. Also, the visibility of cropmarks (see below) tends to vary from year to year. Everything from the time of day, wind speed, cloud cover, altitude and the angle at which the photographs are taken can affect the quality of the final record.

Archaeological background

The proposed route avoided all upstanding recorded archaeological sites, but the research indicated that sites with no visible surface expression from the ground could be affected given the rich and varied archaeological landscape. Although the evidence for prehistoric activity in the study area is not well represented by upstanding monuments, artefacts recovered from the general area indicated a range of human activity during prehistory. The nature of the finds was also indicative of the sensitivity of certain environments; for example, numerous artefacts were recovered during peat extraction in bog at Clonaddadoran or from the riverbeds of the Nore, Gully and Erkina rivers. Ecclesiastical complexes at Aghaboe and Aghmacart also yielded stone and bronze axeheads.

The majority of recorded monuments along the route date from the fifth century AD or later and are classified as ringforts or enclosures. In the early historic period the entire region of Laois formed part of the provincial kingdom of Leinster (Feehan 1983). From this period it was divided into seven septs, or clans, to form the territory of the Laigis, the people who gave the present county its name. Laigis territory is notable for the number of early monastic sites within its borders, and the creation of these settlements provided a magnet for Viking raids. The enduring legacy of the Anglo-Normans in this region is the masonry castle, 56 of which lie ruined in the landscape of County Laois. The majority of these standing castles are tower houses; examples are those at Granstown, Gortnaclea and Tintore and ruins at Aghmacart.

In general, aerial survey is not much used in relation to reconnaissance and the conservation of the architectural heritage. However, it is becoming routine to conduct aerial surveys of all built heritage—including protected structures, items of architectural heritage merit and the general building stock—along a route to provide a comprehensive record. This is the first time that all-inclusive aerial surveys of such structures have been undertaken. A secondary benefit of such surveys is that this information can inform the interim surveys currently being prepared on a county basis by the Department of the Environment, Heritage and Local Government for the National Inventory of Architectural Heritage.

The aerial surveys undertaken for the scheme informed the archaeological research, led to exciting new discoveries and assisted in the selection of the preferred route. Within this scheme, new sites were revealed along the route, the extent of existing sites was clarified and features of architectural interest were identified. Most importantly, all features and archaeological sites identified by the two aerial surveys were avoided by the final route alignment.

Upstanding monuments

Monuments and sites representing past human activity can be viewed from the air in a number of ways. Structures such as tower houses, castles and churches and earthworks in the form of mounds, motte and baileys etc. are easily detectable and readily viewed. Sites of this type along the route have been documented previously. However, aerial survey is especially useful in determining whether there are any previously unrecorded associated sites and features. In the correct conditions, remains of buried archaeological sites are often

Illus. 4—Aghaboe ecclesiastical complex (RMP No. LA022-019) with possible associated earthworks, February 2002 (Margaret Gowen & Co. Ltd)

visible and the full extent of a site can become apparent. The new information gained about the condition and preservation of individual sites can be added to the files in the Archaeological Survey of Ireland (ASI).

It is important to view a site from different angles and heights to ensure that all associated features are identified and that the site is fully recorded. The bawn (an enclosing feature) of Gortnaclea Castle (Record of Monuments and Places [RMP] No. LA023-016) had been previously recorded only to the south and west of the upstanding castle. From the aerial photography, it was possible to see that this feature fully surrounded the castle (Illus. 3). Other monuments, such as ecclesiastical settlements, can have many different associated elements and are defined as complexes. Owing to the nature of these sites, they are often large in scale, and aerial photography is ideal for identifying their full extent and illustrating how they fit into the existing landscape. Aerial survey was particularly useful in assessing two large ecclesiastical complexes in the environs of the route at Aghmacart (LA034-019) and Aghaboe (LA022-019) and in ensuring that no archaeological features associated with these complexes were impinged on by the route (Illus. 4).

Upstanding sites can often have a low profile or visibility and can appear to be badly damaged or partly destroyed. Such sites are most visible from a low level, at an oblique angle and in the early morning/late evening in wintertime. At Lismore the RMP records a church (in ruins) and a graveyard with headstones dating to 1700 (LA022-018-01 & LA022-018-02). This site is dedicated to St Canice and is known as Kilkennybeg. A tower house is indicated in Lismore on the Down Survey parish maps (dated 1654–6); the two structures indicated on the equivalent barony maps likely represent the tower house and the

107

Illus. 5—Earthwork visible to the south-west of Lismore church and graveyard (RMP Nos LA022-018-01 and LA022-018-02), February 2002 (Margaret Gowen & Co. Ltd)

Illus. 6—Platform north-west of Boston Bridge, which may represent the remains of a burial ground, February 2001 (Margaret Gowen & Co. Ltd)

church. The aerial survey revealed a large, rectangular, low-visibility earthwork (Illus. 5) adjacent to the upstanding graveyard wall. This feature was identified to the south-west, outside of the recorded monument area. It continued into the neighbouring field and was detectable through the discoloration of the ploughsoil as a soilmark. This mark may be indicative of decayed buried features. Both the earthwork and the recorded monument were avoided by the road scheme.

Natural features, such as rivers, are important to assess from a landscape perspective, as they attracted settlement in the past—providing a source of food and an artery for trade and transportation of goods—and also acted as natural boundaries. Reverend William Carrigan (1905) recorded the existence of a small hill, a quarter of an acre in area, in the centre of a bog at Oldglass Bridge, now Boston Bridge. The hilltop was called 'the hill of the yew tree' and reportedly was the site of an ancient burial ground, but no above-ground trace of this was apparent at the turn of the 20th century, according to Carrigan. During the aerial survey a conspicuous raised platform was identified in Kilnaseer townland on the south bank of the River Erkina, upstream of Boston Bridge and c. 100 m west of the realigned road corridor. The site consisted of a roughly semicircular platform, which gently rose to a second, roughly rectangular platform with an uneven surface (Illus. 6). The platform identified during the aerial survey may represent the hill that Carrigan described. It is considered to be of archaeological potential and was avoided by the proposed scheme.

Cropmarks

A number of cropmarks were viewed as part of the M7 Portlaoise–Castletown/M8 Portlaoise–Cullahill Motorway scheme. Cropmarks are caused by variations in the subsoil due to the presence of buried archaeological features, resulting in differential crop growth (Illus. 7 & 8). As the crop begins to ripen in early summer, the buried archaeological features affect the rate at which the crops grow and change colour and the height to which they grow. For example, crop cover over a buried ditch will result in a taller, stronger crop because the ditch will contain additional moisture and more nutrients compared to the surrounding undisturbed subsoil. These are known as 'positive' cropmarks. Conversely, the buried remains of a structure or a wall will encourage water to drain from the soil, resulting in weaker, smaller crops and stunted growth. Such features are referred to as 'negative' cropmarks. Cereal crops, such as wheat and barley, provide good definition and produce the best results for the identification of cropmarks. Weather patterns can also affect the detection rate. Cropmarks are enhanced and become more pronounced during dry weather and are very marked in drought conditions.

Geological features can often be incorrectly interpreted as cropmarks, and modern agricultural practices also form patterns that add confusion about the true nature of a newly detected feature. However, geological cropmarks may also give useful information about the location and the type of natural landscape in which a site once existed. The use of aerial photography during an Environmental Impact Assessment (EIA) complements field visits on the ground and helps in the full assessment of the nature of a site. As a surveying instrument, aerial photography is a complementary tool and not a replacement for fieldwork.

Illus. 7—Cropmark of ringfort (RMP No. LA034-029) in Parknahown townland from the south-west, August 2001 (Margaret Gowen & Co. Ltd)

New discoveries at Parknahown and Oldtown

There is a cluster of recorded monuments and newly revealed sites at the southern end of the M8 leg of the scheme in the townlands of Parknahown and Oldtown. In Parknahown the scheme runs through a landscape of significant archaeological potential, suggested by two enclosure sites (LA034-023 & LA034-027) and two ringforts (LA034-028-01 & LA034-029). The landscape here is broadly undulating, with soils suited to productive pasture and tillage. It was noticeable that degradation of the features had taken place since they had been officially inspected as part of the ASI in 1990 and 1991 and the time of the 2002 aerial survey. In some cases previously upstanding ringforts had been levelled and could be identified only as cropmarks. Two sites are recorded in Parknahown townland, south-east of the route. A ringfort (LA034-029), recorded as a sub-circular area, is marked on the 1841 edition Ordnance Survey 6-inch map. The remains of a bank had been visible when the site was inspected in 1991. This site is now visible only at certain angles from the air as a cropmark (Illus. 7). The second site in this part of the townland was identified through aerial photography conducted by the Cambridge University Committee for Air Photography and is recorded as a cropmark of sub-circular conjoined enclosures (LA034-023). This site was not visible from the ground when inspected by the ASI in 1990 and was not visible from the air when the archaeological aerial survey was conducted for the route selection in 2001. However, during the 2002 aerial survey a site in an adjacent field to the east was identified as a double enclosure (Illus. 8). This site was previously unknown. The benefits of carrying out this second aerial survey were further highlighted by the fact that despite the availability of excellent, 1:3000-scale, vertical aerial photographs, taken for engineering and survey purposes by BKS Survey Ltd in 2001, none of the recorded or newly revealed archaeological features could be identified from this source.

Illus. 8—Newly identified double enclosure in Parknahown townland to the east of an enclosure site (RMP LA034-023), February 2002 (Margaret Gowen & Co. Ltd)

Illus. 9—Three newly identified cropmark sites in Oldtown townland from the north-west, August 2001 (Margaret Gowen & Co. Ltd)

Although the main alignment of the M7/M8 route avoids all previously recorded monuments, the archaeological potential of the area suggested by the concentration of recorded and newly identified sites in Parknahown was borne out by the identification of three circular or oval cropmarks in the neighbouring townland of Oldtown (Illus. 9). The cropmarks were in a large cultivated field; the northern half of which was relatively level. The southern half of the field was dominated by three knolls, each of which, on aerial survey, revealed the cropmark of an enclosure, including a bivallate (double ditch) enclosure on the central rise. The two univallate (single ditch) enclosures measured 38 m by 38 m (Site C) and 38 m by 39 m (Site A); the bivallate enclosure measured 61 m by 58 m (Site B). The ringfort (LA034-02801) in Parknahown, to the north, and a ringfort (LA034-034) in Oldtown, to the south-west, are both visible from the summit of the knolls and may be contemporary with the enclosures. Alternatively, the enclosures may pre-date the early medieval period or may have been used over an extended period.

Geophysical survey was undertaken by John Nicholls to confirm the extent of the cropmarks in Oldtown and to identify potentially associated features or additional sites. This survey identified a fourth (Site D) and possibly a fifth partial enclosure (Site E), along with numerous linear and pit-type features that may be archaeological (Illus. 10). The scheme was successfully redesigned to avoid direct impact on all of the newly identified enclosure sites.

The results of the geophysical survey were used to determine a test excavation strategy to assess the nature, complexity and extent of the potential archaeological features in the area affected by the motorway scheme. With the application of a specialised testing strategy devised for this sensitive landscape, the new road alignment was topsoil stripped under archaeological supervision and then investigated. No further archaeological sites were revealed, confirming the results of the aerial and geophysical surveys.

Conclusion

The benefits of archaeological aerial survey as an important research tool have long been recognised by archaeologists. For large-scale, linear infrastructural projects such as road schemes, aerial survey is an ideal technique to examine the potential impact of a proposed scheme on the cultural heritage of an area. By providing a more holistic perspective on the extent and location of sites and monuments, this method allows the broader landscape to be examined during the route selection phase and the EIA. The cost-effective, rapid collection and presentation of these visual data allow project archaeologists to understand and appreciate the archaeological potential of a proposed scheme to a greater degree.

While the benefits of using this technique are many, it must be realised that there are limiting factors. Aerial survey is weather dependent, and it can prove difficult to schedule a flight to tie in with other work on the scheme and general project time constraints. There is great potential to reveal additional sites in pasture or arable land at certain times of year; however, the survey can be of limited use in other terrain such as bogland, forestry or land with heavy vegetation. Furthermore, the true status of the features and cropmarks identified during the aerial survey can be revealed only through further archaeological examination on the ground.

In the case of the M7 Portlaoise–Castletown/M8 Portlaoise–Cullahill Motorway scheme the use of aerial survey has led to a greater knowledge of the extent of recorded

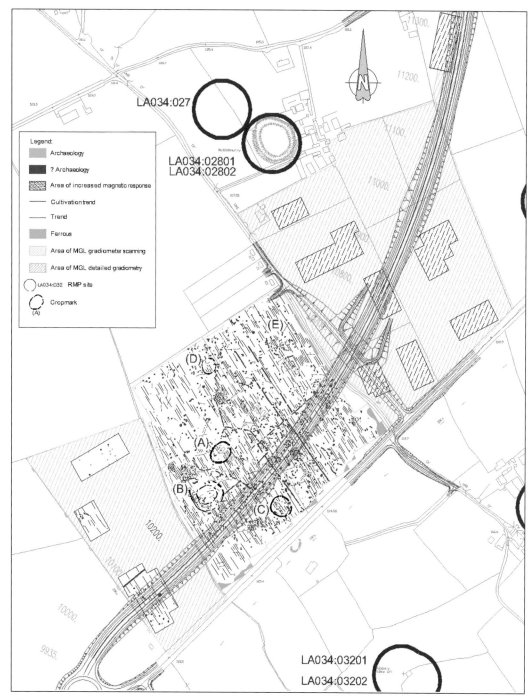

Illus. 10—Final route alignment through Oldtown townland with geophysical interpretative drawing (Margaret Gowen & Co. Ltd, based on the Ordnance Survey Ireland map)

archaeological sites and to the identification, recording and avoidance of a number of previously unidentified archaeological sites and complexes. Importantly, this work at the design stage of the project avoided the need for archaeological excavation in some key areas.

Acknowledgements

Thanks to Sylvia Desmond and Noel Dunne, project archaeologists with Kildare County Council National Roads Design Office, who managed and advised on this scheme. The aerial surveys were funded by the National Roads Authority and Laois County Council. Thanks also to all those at Margaret Gowen & Co. Ltd, especially Siobhán Deery for providing some of the aerial photographs and Kieron Goucher for all of the illustrations. I would also like to acknowledge and thank Marion Sutton who researched the EIS report, which formed the basis of the archaeological background section.

11. Death, decay and reconstruction: the archaeology of Ballykilmore cemetery, County Westmeath

John Channing and Patrick Randolph-Quinney

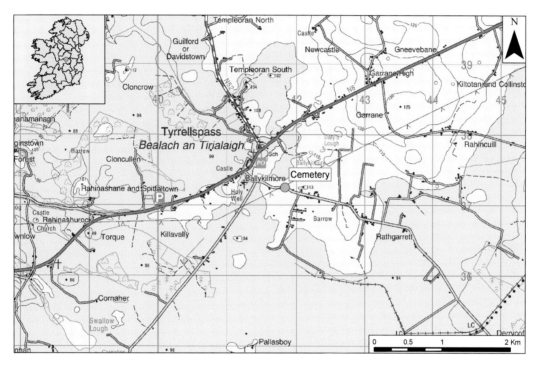

Illus. 1—Location map of Ballykilmore cemetery, Co. Westmeath (based on the Ordnance Survey Ireland map)

A medieval cemetery was discovered in Ballykilmore townland, Co. Westmeath (NGR 241842, 237245; height 113 m OD; ministerial direction no. A001-032), some 800 m south of the village of Tyrrellspass, alongside and beneath the existing Tyrrellspass–Croghan road (Illus. 1). The site was discovered by Cultural Resource Development Services Ltd during centreline testing (excavation licence no. 04E0879) during advance archaeological works for the new N6 Kinnegad to Kilbeggan dual carriageway. Excavation of the site was conducted by Valerie J Keeley Ltd on behalf of Westmeath County Council and was funded by the National Roads Authority (NRA) under the National Development Plan, 2000–2006. The site lay on a ridge of glacial gravel (an esker). (The highest point of this ridge was east of the site.) It was defined by a curvilinear ditched enclosure that straddled the west of the ridge. The ditch probably enclosed an area of c. 7700 m², within which the structural remains of a possible church, metalworking areas, and human burials were found (Illus. 2). This paper presents a provisional interpretation of the site, as the field records, finds and samples are currently undergoing post-excavation analysis. A full presentation of archaeological findings and osteological results will be published after completion of this work.

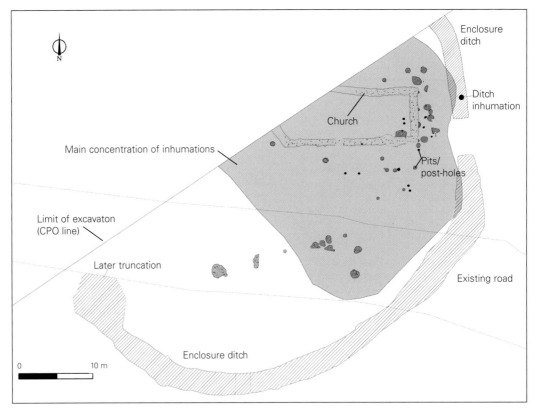

Illus. 2—Schematic diagram of Ballykilmore cemetery (Valerie J Keeley Ltd)

Excavation of the cemetery

The enclosure

The enclosing ditch had a V-shaped profile with a slightly rounded base. An entrance causeway, some 2 m wide, broke the ditch line at its eastern extent. The surviving width of the ditch varied between 2 m and 3.3 m; it was narrowest at the entrance terminals. The surviving ditch varied between 1.47 m and 1.61 m in depth. Circumstantial evidence supports the former existence of an internal bank with a similar circumference to the ditch. The ditch fill consisted of three broad groupings: (1) initial silting up, followed by (2) deliberate backfilling and, finally, (3) all surface expression being removed through agricultural processes. Two pits (one of which may have been used for *in situ* metalworking) and 10 later burials were cut into the ditch backfill.

Internal structures

The drystone wall foundations of a rectangular structure with an east–west alignment were found at the eastern edge of the enclosure interior. This lay some 5 m from the enclosure ditch, partly in front of the entrance causeway, and was built on gently sloping ground. The eastern wall measured 7.3 m long externally, and the southern wall was 20.71 m long. The north-west corner lay outside the area of archaeological investigation. The width of the foundations varied between 0.98 m and 1.25 m, with a surviving depth of cut of between 0.09 m and 0.37 m.

116

Owing to truncation of the interior of the building by burials and robbing of stone from the foundation trenches, it was not possible to identify a floor or construction surface conclusively. A general spread of irregular stones sealed the foundation trenches and most of the surrounding adult burials. However, there were occasional inhumations both on the surface of and within the stone spread. The structure enclosed multiple burials, directly truncating 12 of them, and was itself overlain by several later infant burials. Without a clear floor surface it is not possible to identify categorically which internal burials pre-/post-dated or were contemporary with the structure. The structure is provisionally interpreted as a church.

Internal features
Elsewhere in the interior of the enclosure—in particular close to the stone foundations—pits and post-holes suggested the presence of other timber-built structures, with associated domestic and iron-working activities. The pits contained evidence of both redeposited ferrous metalworking residues and domestic waste (such as butchered animal bone and charcoal). However, the intensity of truncation by later burials meant that no complete structures could be identified.

Finds
The site produced very few artefacts. The finds assemblage was dominated by coffin nails, shroud pins, and 18th- or 19th-century ceramics, together with occasional medieval and early post-medieval pottery sherds. Flint artefacts were recovered, including a single thumbnail scraper, some debitage (waste flakes), and a possible core (a stone from which flakes are struck). The site assemblage also contained cut stone (possibly from a window moulding), glass beads, a bone comb fragment, and a range of ferrous metal objects, including knife blades and an arrowhead (Illus. 3). In general, the finds are not well provenanced, coming from redeposited contexts such as grave fills or topsoil.

The cemetery population

Over 900 'burial events' could be identified within the limits of excavation (Table 1), varying from individual graves (c. 817) to discrete clusters of reburied bone (c. 85), together with a large quantity of disarticulated bone, including butchered faunal remains. Further burials remain preserved *in situ* outside the northern limit of the roadtake. The population of the Ballykilmore cemetery would have been significantly greater than the number of inhumations excavated, perhaps in the order of 1,500 individuals. Of the 800 or so intact or surviving inhumations, a provisional minimum of three burial phases was recognised:
1. Phase 1 (Illus. 4a) comprised burials that were predominantly east–west in alignment. These were mainly unlined graves with frequent use of stone head supports and no grave goods. Many of these were flexed (knees drawn up toward the chest and the back straight). This first phase may be contemporary with the cutting of the enclosure ditch and almost certainly pre-dates the foundation of the stone church.
2. Phase 2 (Illus. 4b) comprised burials that were mainly east–west inhumations; many of these were directly aligned with the stone church. In the main they were extended, supine inhumations (resting on the back with the face upward), often multiple. Some

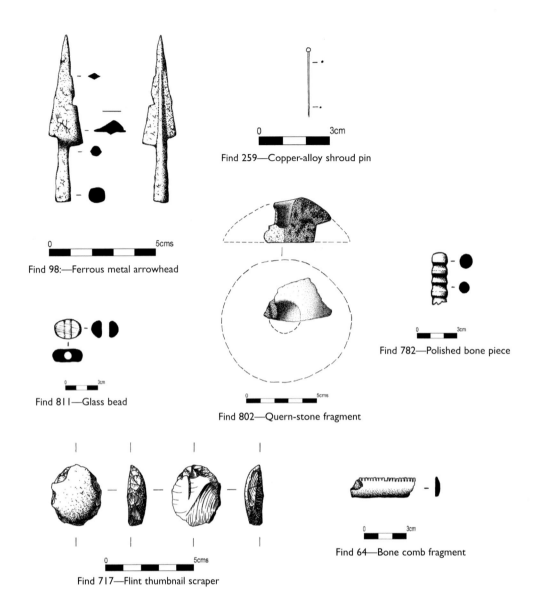

Find 259—Copper-alloy shroud pin

Find 98:—Ferrous metal arrowhead

Find 782—Polished bone piece

Find 811—Glass bead

Find 802—Quern-stone fragment

Find 64—Bone comb fragment

Find 717—Flint thumbnail scraper

Illus. 3—A selection of finds from Ballykilmore cemetery (Valerie J Keeley Ltd)

individuals were buried within coffins or in loosely stone-lined graves with the use of stone head supports (and very occasionally using skulls from other burials as supports).

3. Phase 3 (Illus. 4c) represents the informal use of the burial ground as a *cillín*, or unconsecrated burial ground. The inhumations were predominantly those of neonates (babies from birth to four weeks) and infants, with wide variation in alignment, body position and burial depth. Some of the infants were buried in wooden coffins, though most were uncoffined or wrapped in shrouds fixed at the head with copper-alloy pins.

Analysis of burial orientations suggests that more than one church may have existed on the site and that several successive structures were built, culminating in the stone building described here. The vast majority of Phase 1 and 2 burials were orientated around 270°

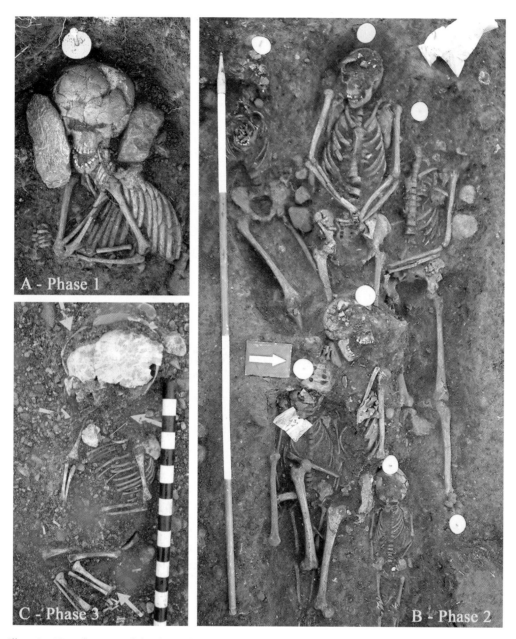

Illus. 4—Typical images of the three phases of use of the cemetery: (a) Phase 1, flexed child inhumation; (b) Phase 2, multiple burial cluster; (c) Phase 3, cillín *burial with shroud pins (arrowed) (Valerie J Keeley Ltd)*

Table 1—Quantification of bone clusters and inhumations by provisional age group

Age group	Bone cluster	Inhumation	Total
Perinate/neonate	7	148	155
Infant/child	18	296	314
Juvenile	11	95	106
Adult	19	276	295
Unassigned	30	2	32
Total	85	817	902

(east–west), with the majority clustered around the alignment of the church. However, sub-clusters were noted at 240° and 255° (WSW–ENE), which may have been aligned on earlier wooden buildings, although convincing evidence for this did not survive.

The reconstruction of burial events

The most common archaeological finds encountered at Ballykilmore were human skeletal remains. It may seem strange to write of human bones as archaeological 'finds', but the act of burial is a cultural one—as the dead do not bury themselves—and is often imbued with ritual and symbolism that the archaeologist attempts to understand in the same way as other aspects of material culture (Parker Pearson 1999, 197). Traditionally, the osteoarchaeologist was recruited for post-excavation analysis and would rarely be involved in the excavation process or interpretation of the archaeological sequence. Today it is recognised that much information is lost if the bone specialist is not directly involved in the recovery process. Rather than simply reporting on the biology of the bone assemblage after the skeletons have been lifted, the specialist can directly influence interpretation of archaeological deposits on-site (Saul & Saul 2002). With this in mind, we here discuss how the osteoarchaeologist (Randolph-Quinney) and archaeologist (Channing) working together can bring additional insights to our study of past behaviour.

Osteoarchaeology is loosely defined as the specialised study of human behaviour through skeletal remains. These are not simply 'dry bone' but represent the end product of a complex series of interactions, some genetic, some environmental, that record bio-cultural information about life history. As such, they tend to inform about the life of an individual rather than the manner of their death. Osteological analysis can provide us with information about the biological sex of an individual, their age at death, how tall and well built they were, what diseases they may have suffered from, their ancestry and the geographical region of their upbringing, and very rarely, the manner or cause of their death. (For an excellent example of skeletal analysis in practice as part of NRA road projects see Fibiger 2005.)

Archaeology is often compared to detective work, with an excavation and a crime scene being seen as similar in many ways. At each, investigators attempt to reconstruct and interpret a past event through the preservation, recovery and interpretation of physical evidence, a major difference being the time-scale of the events and the delay since they occurred. In both forms of investigation it is now realised that understanding the processes of decay, decomposition, and skeletonisation of human remains can be a powerful tool in our interpretation of past events; this investigation is generally referred to as taphonomy. Taphonomy was first applied to palaeontological sites, the term being derived from *taphos* (burial), and *nomos* (law). Subsequently, it has been applied to a wide range of studies in archaeology and forensics and deals with patterns of bias, damage, dispersal and/or accumulation of bones or other clastic components (transportable elements such as stone tool debitage) in the soil in an attempt to infer their depositional history in greater detail. The use of such data has shed significant light on funerary behaviour and treatment of the dead at Ballykilmore.

Of particular interest is evidence for primary versus secondary deposition of human remains. Primary deposition concerns the initial location in which the body is placed; the recognition of a primary context indicates an undisturbed context and one that records a

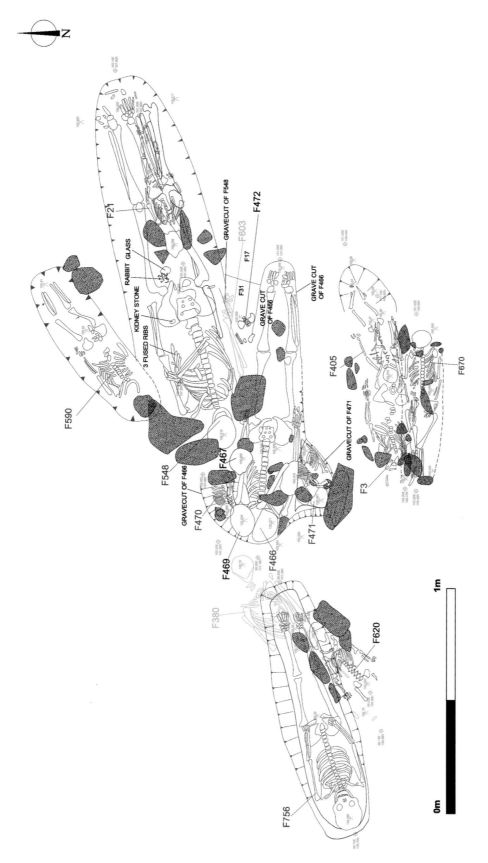

N

F21

GRAVECUT OF F548

F603

F472

F17

F31

GRAVE CUT
OF F466

GRAVE CUT
OF F466

RABBIT GLASS

KIDNEY STONE

3 FUSED RIBS

F405

F670

F590

GRAVECUT OF F471

F548

GRAVECUT OF F466

F467

F3

F470

F471

F469

F466

F380

F620

F756

1m

0m

Illus. 5—Plan of the Phase 2 complex burial cluster (Valerie J Keeley Ltd)

Illus. 6—(a) Adult female burial (left) cut by later adult male inhumation; (b) the female burial after excavation of the male burial (Valerie J Keeley Ltd)

high level of contextual information. Secondary deposition occurs when remains are removed from the site of initial deposition and redeposited elsewhere; contextual information relating to the original depositional environment is usually lost, and the remains tend to be out of anatomical position and invariably winnowed with respect to smaller skeletal elements such as hand and foot bones. In general, there was intense competition for burial space at the Ballykilmore site. The area used for interments seems to have been restricted (Illus. 2), either by social proscription or by a physical boundary. This limitation forced the reuse of existing burial plots, with the effect that earlier, primary burials were disturbed or truncated by later ones. This is clearly shown by Illus. 5, in which 14 sequential burials were intercut and commingled within an area of just under 5 m². Such intensity of ground use was not uncommon across the site.

The deposition of secondary contexts seems to have been largely expedient. Later burials cut through earlier ones, with some or all of the disturbed material being placed back into the grave fill of the truncating burial. This is demonstrated in Illustration 6, where the primary burial of a young adult female (left) was truncated by the intrusion of a young

Illus. 7—Burial showing articulated neck vertebrae in situ (Valerie J Keeley Ltd)

adult male (right). After excavation of the later burial, the damage to the female skeleton can clearly be seen: the majority of her left side has been truncated and removed. The disturbed left-side humerus, radius, femur and fibula of the woman were placed in their approximate anatomical position within the grave of the man, with the remaining truncated parts (primarily bones of the hands and feet) dispersed randomly through the grave fill.

Analysis of the pattern of damage to the young woman's remains indicates that the individual was most likely fully skeletonised when the truncation took place and had therefore been interred for a considerable time before disturbance. This is indicated by the nature of spade damage to the remaining *in situ* skeletal parts. A small portion of the medial border of the left shoulder blade and the vertebral ends of the left ribs remained undisturbed within the grave fill. These had been cleanly cut with transverse fractures, indicating impact to dry bone, the bone subsequently remaining in its anatomical position. If truncation had occurred when the individual was fleshed, the resulting spatial distribution would have been different. In the latter case, the presence of soft tissue around bone creates a void-space as decomposition proceeds; the bones within remain in an unstable position until decay has finished and the surrounding void is filled with soil. If truncation had occurred while the bones were unsupported by soil then a degree of disarticulation and dispersal would be evident in the remaining tissues as a consequence of spade impact.

A variant on the theme of secondary deposition, this time before full skeletonisation, was recorded in another burial, where the disarticulated and semi-articulated remains of at least three individuals were recovered. Of note was a fragmented adult male skull under which lay five articulated cervical (neck) vertebrae arranged vertically (Illus. 7). (In general, the neck vertebrae below the second cervical element tend to remain articulated for a longer period than other parts of the skeleton, due to strong ligament attachments and complex interlocking surfaces, whereas the first and second cervical vertebrae, and the

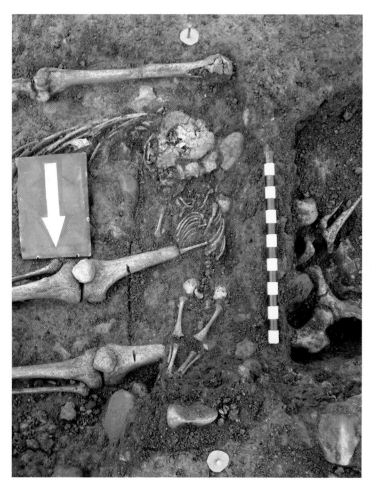

Illus. 8—Perinatal burial deposited onto legs of earlier, adult inhumation (Valerie J Keeley Ltd)

hands and arms tend to be the first areas to undergo disarticulation (Roksandic 2002).) These directly overlay an articulated left elbow and wrist joint, probably derived from the same individual. The articulated nature of these anatomical parts suggests that they were derived from a primary deposit while still bearing flesh, muscle or connective tissue and were probably disinterred within the first year or two of burial (Galloway 1997; Rodriguez 1997). This highlights the competition for burial space that took place, with the removal of body parts from recently disturbed earth during the process of digging fresh graves. It is possible that such competition may have been brought about during times of 'plague or pestilence' when local death rates may have soared, prompting rapid reuse of the burial ground.

The Ballykilmore grave-diggers sometimes respected the position of an underlying primary burial when cutting later graves, as shown in Illustration 8, where, in attempting to cut a grave for a perinatal (newborn) burial, they encountered the legs of an earlier, adult inhumation. The spade marks of the grave-digger are clearly evidenced just above the knee joints of the adult; the digger obviously decided to cut no deeper into the earlier burial and deposited the infant remains directly onto the skeletonised legs of the adult.

Finally, we have evidence for casual disposal of the dead. In this example a well-preserved adult burial was discovered within the upper layers of the enclosure ditch (Illus. 9a), with no grave cut discernible. The inhumation was orientated roughly east–west, with the head to the west. The remains were those of a young adult female of relatively short

Illus. 9—(a) Young adult female deposited in the upper fill of the ditch; (b) foetal bone cluster within the maternal pelvis; (c) articulated foetal remains in situ *outside and below the maternal pelvis* (Valerie J Keeley Ltd)

stature (1.53 m). The body was deposited in an extended supine position, with the upper body and torso at a higher level than the lower body. The pitch and inclination of the inhumation generally reflected the profile of the surrounding ditch at the same level. The disposition of the body was irregular. Although the burial was supine and extended, the right arm was highly flexed, lying over and above the skull, with the metacarpal (palm) bones preserving a flexed position; the right phalanges (finger bones) were slightly dispersed but generally reflected the curled aspect of the hand. The left arm was lightly flexed and splayed away from the torso; the bones of the left hand were disarticulated and dispersed, being recovered at a lower level adjacent to the left hip. The placement of the body is consistent with the dumping of the corpse into the silted up enclosure ditch without a formal grave being dug. From a taphonomic perspective, the relative lack of skeletal element dispersal (particularly the right hand), together with the condition of the remains, suggests that the body was covered with a soil mantle after being deposited into the ditch. Why was the body treated in such a casual and disrespectful way?

The answer may lie in the discovery of the partial skeleton of a foetus within the pelvic cavity of the young woman. The bones recovered comprised fragmented cranial squama (skull vault bones), parts of the pelvis, and the long bones of the legs; the leg bones were orientated with their proximal (upper) ends pointing toward the maternal head (Illus. 9b). After excavation of the foetal and adult remains, a second cluster of infant bones was found some 0.15 m to the south and just below the level of the adult pelvis. These remains were found in an extended prone position (face downward), head orientated toward the maternal pelvis, with the bones arrayed in near-anatomical position (Illus. 9c).

The spatial disposition of the clusters would at first suggest the presence of two individuals, with the lower limbs of the foetus within the maternal pelvis pointing towards the mother's head, and the upper limbs, torso and skull of a second infant (also pointing in the same direction) fully articulated outside the pelvis. However, analysis of the two bone groups indicates that there was no replication of anatomical parts between the sets of remains, and conjoins were possible between broken cranial squama of the foetus found within the adult pelvis and the skull of the infant found outside it. This indicates that the two assemblages comprised parts of the same individual, which were determined to have been between 35 weeks *intra uterine* (in the womb) and full term at death. The spatial disjunction between the two groups can be explained through decomposition processes and post-mortem changes in the soft tissues of the mother (Clark et al. 1997; Gill-King 1997). In this instance, portions of the infant were left inside the mother, in addition to the articulated remains found outside the pelvis.

This highlights one of the problems facing archaeologists when attempting to determine whether a mother and infant died in childbirth. The presence of foetal bones within the birth canal, irrespective of their spatial orientation, does not unequivocally indicate that death occurred during the birth process, given that foetal tissue can migrate towards the low point of the pelvis or the outlet, as appears to have been the case here. Owing to these taphonomic considerations we cannot with certainty say whether the mother and child died during birthing, but we can say that the mother was heavily pregnant at the time of her death.

The motivation behind the dumping of her body may relate to a number of social factors on which we can only speculate. Was her rough and ready post-mortem treatment a result of the fact that she died in or close to childbirth, due to the paternity of her child, because she was diseased and feared contagious, or because of some other segregating factor relating to her social standing or physical appearance? Although no evidence of infectious disease was noted on her skeleton, many pathogens such as influenza, typhus and cholera do not leave skeletal lesions, while others such as tuberculosis, syphilis and leprosy may manifest themselves skeletally only in chronic cases. She did, however, display pronounced shape abnormality of the skull, with the vault very long and low, with the formation of multiple bony platelets between the major bones making up the back of the skull (Illus. 10). This is consistent with craniostenosis, a congenital abnormality of unspecific cause whereby cranial vault bones fuse together at a premature age (usually <7 years), leading to distortion along the trajectory of continuing cranial development.

It is likely that the burial dates from the final, *cillín* phase of the cemetery, and the act highlights the fact that unconsecrated burial grounds were not used solely for stillborn or unbaptised infants. Such sites were also used for adult burials of individuals whose manner of death might be considered 'abnormal' or socially unacceptable (see Nolan, this volume). This included suicides, murder victims, drowning victims, persons of unknown religion and women who died in childbirth. The last category may have been the reason behind the disrespectful treatment of this young woman, although it is worth noting that there are several other cases at Ballykilmore of burials with full-term infants in similar pelvic positions. These individuals were buried conventionally within the consecrated zone of the burial ground, although, given the taphonomic issues surrounding such burials, we cannot be certain in these instances that the cause of death was in any way birth related.

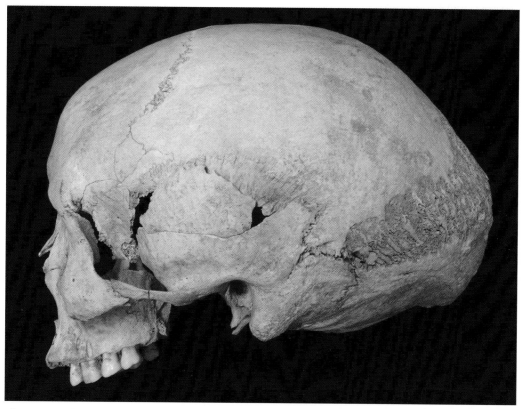

Illus. 10—Side view of the skull of the female ditch burial, showing long and low profile and the formation of multiple bony platelets between the major bones comprising the back of the skull (Valerie J Keeley Ltd)

Conclusions

The Ballykilmore cemetery highlights the seemingly informal use of burial space and disrespectful treatment of the dead during the medieval period. (Radiocarbon dates are awaited at the time of writing but should confirm the broadly medieval date of the burials.) This runs counter to the modern preconception of what a Christian burial ground should look like, with formal, well-tended graves and an air of solemnity. In context, Ballykilmore fits very well with what archaeologists and historians have come to understand of pre-modern treatment of the dead and social use of burial space.

In medieval Europe the realities of illness and death were an everyday part of life. Adult life expectancy was considerably less than today, and infant mortality was enormous. During times of war, famine and plague, death was ubiquitous. The dead were an accepted part of the living community, and, as Leigh Fry (1999, 47) has pointed out, 'in a time when houses were tiny and crowded and streets were narrow, muddy and filthy, the cemetery served as the town's public space. The cemetery—rather than being removed from the daily life of the living community—was at its centre.' Rather than being solemn, segregated places, medieval Irish cemeteries displayed a closeness between the living and dead almost unknown today, being used for fairs and markets, as locations to make contracts and swear oaths, as places of shelter, and to graze cattle.

A strong tradition of respect for noble and elite graves and tombs existed, but the general state of non-elite burial grounds seems to have been poor, although it must be noted that, however badly the burial environment was maintained, compassion for the individual dead at Ballykilmore was obviously still important. Our analyses point to the repeated use of single graves, with later generations of burials successively interred within the same cut, possibly indicating familial ties. Many of the graves clearly show the time and effort invested in their construction, with great care being taken in the placement of the bodies within, whether coffin-contained, shroud-wrapped or unenclosed. In the vast majority of cases, bodies were not simply dumped into graves, or left for the attentions of the elements and scavengers, but were treated with respect and deference.

Acknowledgements

We would like to thank the Ballykilmore excavation crew and support staff of Valerie J Keeley Ltd, Westmeath County Council archaeologists Rónán Swan (project archaeologist) and Orlaith Egan (assistant project archaeologist) for their help during the excavation, Sinéad Doyle for preparation of the line drawings, Dr Tim Young for advice on site archaeometallurgy, and Jennifer Randolph-Quinney for her comments on an earlier draft of this paper.

Appendix 1—Radiocarbon dates from excavated archaeological sites described in these proceedings

Notes

1. Radiocarbon ages are quoted in conventional years BP (before AD 1950), and the errors for these dates are expressed at the one-sigma (68% probability) level of confidence.

2. Calibrated date ranges are equivalent to the probable calendrical age of the sample material and are expressed at one-sigma (68% probability) and two-sigma (95% probability) levels of confidence.

3. Dates obtained from Beta Analytic in Florida (Beta lab code) were calibrated using the IntCal98 calibration programme (Stuiver et al. 1998). Dates obtained from Waikato Laboratory, New Zealand (Wk lab code), were calibrated using the OxCal v.3.10 calibration programme (Bronk Ramsey 2005) in the case of sites on the N2 Finglas–Ashbourne road scheme (chapters 4 and 8) and using the IntCal04 calibration programme (Reimer et al. 2004) in the case of Monanny, Co. Monaghan. Dates obtained from Queen's University, Belfast (UB lab code), were calibrated using the CALIB 5.0.2 calibration programme (Stuiver et al. 2005). Dates obtained from the Oxford Radiocarbon Accelerator Unit (OxA lab code) were calibrated using the OxCal v.3.5 calibration programme (Bronk Ramsey 2000).

Lab Code	Site	Sample/context	Yrs BP	Calibrated date ranges
Chapter 2 (F Walsh)—Neolithic Monanny, Co. Monaghan				
Wk-17338	Monanny 1	Oak (*Quercus* sp) charcoal from burnt post in west wall of House A	5037 ± 40	3950–3830 BC one sigma 3960–3710 BC two sigma
Wk-17339	Monanny 1	Blackthorn (*Prunus spinosa*) and ash (*Fraxinus excelsior*) charcoal from Bronze Age pit	2705 ± 58	900–805 BC one sigma 1000–790 BC two sigma
Wk-17340	Monanny 1	Blackthorn (*Prunus spinosa*), apple/pear (Pomoideae) and hazel (*Corylus avellana*) charcoal from early medieval cereal-drying kiln	1512 ± 39	AD 530–610 one sigma AD 430–640 two sigma
Wk-17341	Monanny 1	Oak (*Quercus* sp) charcoal from internal wall of House B	5048 ± 40	3950–3790 BC one sigma 3960–3760 BC two sigma

Lab Code	Site	Sample/context	Yrs BP	Calibrated date ranges
Wk-17342	Monanny 1	Oak (*Quercus* sp) charcoal from burnt timber in south wall of House B	5082 ± 64	3880–3790 BC one sigma 3990–3700 BC two sigma
Wk-17343	Monanny 1	Oak (*Quercus* sp) charcoal from burnt post in south wall of House C	5043 ± 43	3950–3830 BC one sigma 3960–3710 BC two sigma
Wk-17344	Monanny 1	Oak (*Quercus* sp) charcoal from burnt post at north-west corner of House C	4991 ± 47	3800–3700 BC one sigma 3950–3650 BC two sigma
Wk-17345	Monanny 1	Oak (*Quercus* sp) plank at base of trough of burnt mound	3221 ± 122	1670–1380 BC one sigma 1900–1100 BC two sigma
Wk-17347	Monanny 1	Oat (*Avena* sp) grain from early medieval cereal-drying kiln	1546 ± 35	AD 430–490 one sigma AD 420–600 two sigma
Wk-17348	Monanny 1	Medieval skeleton, 5 g of femur	761 ± 33	AD 1225–1280 one sigma AD 1215–1290 two sigma

Chapter 3 (D Murphy & S Rathbone)—Early medieval watermill at Killoteran, Co. Waterford

Beta-191530	Killoteran 9	Yew (*Taxus*) post from upper dam	1530 ± 60	AD 440–610 one sigma AD 410–650 two sigma
Beta-191531	Killoteran 9	Oak (*Quercus*) plank from upper dam	1600 ± 60	AD 400–540 one sigma AD 340–600 two sigma

Chapter 4 (M FitzGerald)—Archaeological discoveries on the N2, Counties Meath & Dublin

Wk-15499	Muckerstown, Site 13b	Willow (*Salix*) artefact from large waterlogged pit/well	2990 ± 40	1520–1310 BC one sigma 1600–1210 BC two sigma
Wk-16279	Muckerstown, Site 13b	Ash (*Fraxinus*) charcoal from a stone-lined industrial feature	2175 ± 38	360–170 BC one sigma 380–110 BC two sigma
Wk-16280	Muckerstown, Site 13b	Hazel (*Corylus*) charcoal from drainage feature	1146 ± 52	AD 780–980 one sigma AD 770–1020 two sigma
Wk-16281	Muckerstown, Site 13b	Blackthorn (*Prunus spinosa*) charcoal from small bowl-shaped pit	1055 ± 68	AD 890–1030 one sigma AD 810–1160 two sigma
Wk-16818	Muckerstown, Site 13b	Brushwood panel of hazel (*Corylus*) from large waterlogged pit/well	2990 ± 40	1310–1130 BC one sigma 1390–1080 BC two sigma
Wk-16282	Baltrasna, Site 14	Ash (*Fraxinus*) charcoal from pit	3733 ± 40	2200–2040 BC one sigma 2290–2020 BC two sigma

Lab Code	Site	Sample/context	Yrs BP	Calibrated date ranges
Wk-16284	Baltrasna, Site 17/18	Blackthorn (*Prunus spinosa*) charcoal from large pit	2288 ± 35	400–230 BC one sigma 410–200 BC two sigma
Wk-16286	Baltrasna, Site 17/18	Ash (*Fraxinus*) charcoal from pit	2900 ± 47	1200–1000 BC one sigma 1260–930 BC two sigma
Wk-16287	Baltrasna, Site 17/18	Alder (*Alnus*) vessel or mether	663 ± 36	AD 1280–1390 one sigma AD 1270–1400 two sigma
Wk-16288	Harlockstown, Site 19	Alder (*Alnus*) charcoal from circular enclosure ditch	3515 ± 45	1900–1760 BC one sigma 1960–1690 BC two sigma
Wk-16289	Harlockstown, Site 19	Blackthorn (*Prunus spinosa*) from small barrow	2057 ± 40	160 BC–AD 120 one sigma 180 BC–AD 30 two sigma
Wk-16290	Harlockstown, Site 19	Human bone (right fibula diaphysis fragment) from articulated burial inside circular enclosure	3599 ± 36	2020–1900 BC one sigma 2120–1870 BC two sigma
Wk-16311	Ballybin/Killegland, Site 22	Alder (*Alnus*) charcoal layer of kiln	2016 ± 39	60 BC–AD 50 one sigma 160 BC–AD 700 two sigma
Wk-16313	Cookstown, Site 25	Oak (*Quercus*) and blackthorn (*Prunus spinosa*) charcoal from fill of inner ring-ditch from a complex of two concentric ring-ditches	2148 ± 47	360–100 BC one sigma 360–50 BC two sigma
Wk-16314	Cookstown, Site 25	Blackthorn (*Prunus spinosa*) charcoal from fill of inner ring-ditch from a complex of two concentric ring-ditches	2192 ± 40	360–190 BC one sigma 390–160 BC two sigma
Wk-16316	Rath, Site 27	Ash (*Fraxinus*) vessel from large waterlogged pit	2203 ± 36	360–200 BC one sigma 380–180 BC two sigma
Wk-16317	Rath, Site 27	Oak (*Quercus*) charcoal from ring-ditch containing faience beads	2353 ± 41	510–380 BC one sigma 740–360 BC two sigma
Wk-16320	Rath, Site 27	Alder (*Alnus*) charcoal from large waterlogged pit	2190 ± 35	360–190 BC one sigma 380–160 BC two sigma
Wk-16824	Rath, Site 27	Ash (*Fraxinus*) vessel from large waterlogged pit	2217 ± 36	370–200 BC one sigma 390–190 BC two sigma

Lab Code	Site	Sample/context	Yrs BP	Calibrated date ranges
Chapter 5 (A Lennon)—Ringfort at Leggetsrath West, Co. Kilkenny				
Beta-205166	Leggetsrath West	Animal bone from inner ditch of ringfort	1350 ± 60	AD 650–700 one sigma AD 610–780 two sigma
Beta-205167	Leggetsrath West	Charred materials from later cereal-drying kiln	900 ± 70	AD 1030–1220 one sigma AD 1000–1270 two sigma
Beta-205168	Leggetsrath West	Charred materials from outer ditch of ringfort	1180 ± 60	AD 780–960 one sigma AD 690–990 two sigma
Beta-205169	Leggetsrath West	Charred materials from earlier cereal-drying kiln	1100 ± 60	AD 890–1000 one sigma AD 790–1030 two sigma
Chapter 7 (F Coyne)—'Plectrum-shaped' enclosure at Newtown, Co. Limerick				
Beta-182313	Newtown A	Holly (*Ilex*) charcoal from slot-trench of figure-of-eight building	1150 ± 70	AD 785–980 one sigma AD 700–1015 two sigma
Beta-182314	Newtown A	Oak (*Quercus*) charcoal from central post-hole of figure-of-eight building	970 ± 120	AD 980–1205 one sigma AD 795–1280 two sigma
Beta-182317	Newtown A	Blackthorn (*Prunus* spp) charcoal from base of enclosure ditch	1090 ± 60	AD 890–1005 one sigma AD 795–1030 two sigma
Beta-182323	Newtown A	Blackthorn (*Prunus* spp) from upper fill of enclosure ditch	840 ± 90	AD 1050–1095 one sigma AD 1010–1300 two sigma
Chapter 8 (M Seaver)—Early medieval settlement at Raystown, Co. Meath				
Wk-16294	Raystown, Site 21	Oak (*Quercus*) charcoal in scorched pit	1284 ± 40	AD 670–770 one sigma AD 650–860 two sigma
Wk-16295	Raystown, Site 21	Oak (*Quercus*) charcoal from backfill of Northern Mill 2	938 ± 32	AD 1030–1160 one sigma AD 1020–1170 two sigma
Wk-16296	Raystown, Site 21	Blackthorn (*Prunus spinosa*) charcoal from fill of hearth/kiln	1151 ± 35	AD 780–970 one sigma AD 770–980 two sigma
Wk-16300	Raystown, Site 21	Burnt oak (*Quercus*) in feature within southern mill complex	1188 ± 37	AD 770–890 one sigma AD 710–970 two sigma
Wk-16302	Raystown, Site 21	Blackthorn (*Prunus spinosa*) and hazel (*Corylus*) charcoal from fill of pit cut by souterrain	1249 ± 53	AD 680–860 one sigma AD 660–890 two sigma

Lab Code	Site	Sample/context	Yrs BP	Calibrated date ranges
Wk-16306	Raystown, Site 21	Human bone from articulated burial within ring-ditch	1528 ± 33	AD 440–590 one sigma AD 430–610 two sigma
Wk-16307	Raystown, Site 21	Human bone from articulated burial within ring-ditch	1334 ± 34	AD 650–770 one sigma AD 640–780 two sigma
Wk-16308	Raystown, Site 21	Human bone from articulated burial cutting ring-ditch	1412 ± 34	AD 610–655 one sigma AD 575–665 two sigma
Wk-16309	Raystown, Site 21	Human bone from articulated burial cutting ring-ditch, with blue glass bead	1130 ± 35	AD 885–975 one sigma AD 780–990 two sigma
Wk-16310	Raystown, Site 21	Human bone from articulated burial outside ring-ditch	1195 ± 34	AD 770–880 one sigma AD 700–950 two sigma
Wk-16819	Raystown, Site 21	Human bone from unusual north–south flexed burial	1574 ± 35	AD 430–540 one sigma AD 410–570 two sigma
Wk-16820a	Raystown, Site 21	Human bone from burial south of ring-ditch	1363 ± 36	AD 640–685 one sigma AD 600–770 two sigma
Wk-16820b	Raystown, Site 21	Human bone from burial south of ring-ditch	1312 ± 38	AD 660–770 one sigma AD 660–780 two sigma
Wk-16821	Raystown, Site 21	Human bone from burial south of ring-ditch	1425 ± 33	AD 605–650 one sigma AD 570–660 two sigma
Wk-16822	Raystown, Site 21	Human bone from burial cutting ring-ditch	1510 ± 34	AD 530–610 one sigma AD 430–640 two sigma
Wk-16823	Raystown, Site 21	Human bone from articulated burial within ring-ditch	1647 ± 33	AD 340–435 one sigma AD 260–540 two sigma
Wk-16825	Raystown, Site 21	Human bone from articulated burial within ring-ditch	1537 ± 34	AD 430–580 one sigma AD 430–600 two sigma
Wk-16826a	Raystown, Site 21	Human bone from articulated burial within ring-ditch	1451 ± 35	AD 580–645 one sigma AD 550–660 two sigma
Wk-16826b	Raystown, Site 21	Human bone from articulated burial within ring-ditch	1482 ± 35	AD 550–615 one sigma AD 460–650 two sigma
Wk-16827	Raystown, Site 21	Human bone from articulated burial within ring-ditch	1491 ± 35	AD 540–610 one sigma AD 440–650 two sigma
Wk-16828	Raystown, Site 21	Human bone from articulated burial within ring-ditch, associated with knife	1496 ± 36	AD 540–610 one sigma AD 440–650 two sigma

Lab Code	Site	Sample/context	Yrs BP	Calibrated date ranges
Wk-17907	Raystown, Site 21	Single oat grain from cereal-drying kiln	1575 ± 30	AD 430–540 one sigma AD 410–560 two sigma
Wk-17908	Raystown, Site 21	Single wheat grain from cereal-drying kiln	1428 ± 30	AD 605–650 one sigma AD 570–660 two sigma
Wk-17909	Raystown, Site 21	Cereal from drying kiln containing unusual burial	1607 ± 37	AD 410–540 one sigma AD 380–550 two sigma
Wk-17910	Raystown, Site 21	Single barley grain from subrectangular enclosure	1295 ± 36	AD 665–770 one sigma AD 650–780 two sigma
Wk-17918	Raystown, Site 21	Human bone from articulated burial	1586 ± 32	AD 420–540 one sigma AD 400–550 two sigma
Wk-17919	Raystown, Site 21	Human bone from articulated burial	1531 ± 31	AD 430–580 one sigma AD 430–600 two sigma
Wk-17920	Raystown, Site 21	Human bone from articulated burial	1524 ± 31	AD 460–600 one sigma AD 430–610 two sigma
Wk-17921	Raystown, Site 21	Human bone from articulated burial	1448 ± 35	AD 590–645 one sigma AD 550–660 two sigma
Wk-17922	Raystown, Site 21	Human bone from articulated burial	1598 ± 36	AD 410–540 one sigma AD 390–550 two sigma
UB-6521	Raystown, Site 21	Oak (*Quercus*) timber from Southern Mill 1	1279 ± 32	AD 681–770 one sigma AD 660–782 two sigma
UB-6522	Raystown, Site 21	Oak (*Quercus*) timber from Southern Mill 4	1315 ± 35	AD 659–765 one sigma AD 653–772 two sigma
UB-6523	Raystown, Site 21	Oak (*Quercus*) timber from Southern Mill 5	1206 ± 35	AD 777–874 one sigma AD 691–935 two sigma
UB-6524	Raystown, Site 21	Oak (*Quercus*) timber from Northern Mill 2	1096 ± 35	AD 896–988 one sigma AD 887–1017 two sigma

Chapter 9 (J Nolan)—Children's burial ground at Tonybaun, Co. Mayo

OxA-13119	Tonybaun	Bone (Skeleton 58) from children's burial ground	254 ± 29	AD 1535–1794 one sigma AD 1522–1947 two sigma
OxA-13120	Tonybaun	Bone (Skeleton 288) from children's burial ground	345 ± 29	AD 1490–1629 one sigma AD 1475–1638 two sigma

Lab Code	Site	Sample/context	Yrs BP	Calibrated date ranges
OxA-13121	Tonybaun	Bone (Skeleton 386) from children's burial ground	312 ± 28	AD 1521–1640 one sigma AD 1489–1647 two sigma
OxA-13122	Tonybaun	Bone (Skeleton 515) from children's burial ground	248 ± 35	AD 1533–1945 one sigma AD 1521–1948 two sigma
OxA-13123	Tonybaun	Bone (Skeleton 517) from children's burial ground	255 ± 32	AD 1531–1795 one sigma AD 1520–1948 two sigma
OxA-13124	Tonybaun	Bone (Skeleton 1141) from children's burial ground	159 ± 30	AD 1670–1949 one sigma AD 1664–1951 two sigma
OxA-13228	Tonybaun	Bone (Skeleton 1166) from children's burial ground	205 ± 25	AD 1656–1946 one sigma AD 1650–1948 two sigma
UB-6763	Tonybaun	Ash (*Fraxinus*) and willow (*Ilex*) charcoal from pit fill of furnace pit F66	2045 ± 33	98 BC–AD 1 one sigma 166 BC–AD 25 two sigma
UB-6764	Tonybaun	Oak (*Quercus*) and willow (*Ilex*) charcoal from lazy bed furrows	1483 ± 34	AD 551–613 one sigma AD 467–648 two sigma
UB-6765	Tonybaun	Oak (*Quercus*) charcoal from fill of furnace pit F214	2309 ± 35	405–363 BC one sigma 477–210 BC two sigma
UB-6766	Tonybaun	Willow (*Ilex*) and hazel (*Corylus*) charcoal from activity layer underlying burials from children's burial ground	1176 ± 33	AD 780–891 one sigma AD 772–969 two sigma
UB-6767	Tonybaun	Willow (*Ilex*) and hazel (*Corylus*) charcoal from metalworking residue underlying burials from children's burial ground	1107 ± 32	AD 895–979 one sigma AD 882–1015 two sigma

References

Aldridge, R B 1969 'Notes on children's burial grounds in Mayo', *Journal of the Royal Society of Antiquaries of Ireland*, Vol. 99, 83–7.

Bailey, D W 1996 'The life, times and works of House 59, Tell Ovcharovo, Bulgaria', *in* T Darvill & J Thomas (eds), *Neolithic Houses in North-west Europe and Beyond*, 143–56. Oxbow Monograph Series 57. Oxbow, Oxford.

Bankoff, A & Winter, F 1979 'A house burning in Serbia', *Archaeology*, Vol. 32, 8–14.

Barrett, G 2002 'Flights of discovery: archaeological air survey in Ireland 1989–2000', *Journal of Irish Archaeology*, Vol. 11, 1–30.

Bhreathnach, E 1999 'Authority and supremacy in Tara and its hinterland c. 950–1200', *Discovery Programme Reports*, No. 5, 1–23. Royal Irish Academy/Discovery Programme, Dublin.

Brady, N in press 'Mills in medieval Ireland: looking beyond design', *in* S Walton (ed.), *Wind and Water: the medieval mill*. Arizona Center for Medieval and Renaissance Studies, Tempe, Arizona, USA.

Bronk Ramsey, C 2000 *OxCal Program v.3.5.* http://www.rlaha.ox.ac.uk/orau/06_01.htm

Bronk Ramsey, C 2005 *OxCal Program v.3.10.* http://www.rlaha.ox.ac.uk/O/oxcal.php

Buckley, V 1986 'Ulster and Oriel souterrains—an indicator of tribal areas?', *Ulster Journal of Archaeology*, Vol. 49, 108–10.

Card, N, Downes, J, Gibson, J & Sharman, P 2005 'Religion and metal working at Mine Howe, Orkney', *Current Archaeology,* Vol. 17, No. 199, 322–7.

Carrigan, Rev. W 1905 *The History and Antiquities of the Diocese of Ossory* (4 vols) [1981 reprint]. Roberts Books and Wellbrook Press, Kilkenny.

Carroll, J 2001 'Glass bangles as a regional development in early medieval Ireland', *in* M Redknapp, N Edwards, S Youngs, A Lane & J Knight (eds), *Pattern and Purpose in Insular Art*, 101–14. Oxbow, Oxford.

Charles-Edwards, T 2000 *Early Christian Ireland.* University of Oxford, Oxford.

Clark, M A, Worrell, M B & Pless, J E 1997 'Postmortem changes in soft tissues', *in* W D Haglund & M H Sorg (eds), 151–64.

Clinton, M 2001 *The Souterrains of Ireland.* Wordwell, Bray.

Cooney, G 2000 *Landscapes of Neolithic Ireland.* Routledge, London and New York.

Cooney, G, O'Sullivan, M & Downey, L 2006 *Archaeology 2020: repositioning Irish archaeology in the knowledge society.* University College Dublin, Dublin.

Cotter, E 2000 'Loughboy', *in* I Bennett (ed.), *Excavations 1998: summary accounts of archaeological excavations in Ireland*, 123–4. Wordwell, Bray.

Coyne, F & Collins, T 2003 'Plectrum-shaped enclosures—a new site type at Newtown, Co. Limerick?', *Archaeology Ireland*, Vol. 17, No. 4, 17–19.

Crombie, D 1988 'Children's burial grounds in the Barony of Dunmore: a preliminary note', *Journal of the Galway Archaeological and Historical Society*, Vol. 41, 149–51.

Delaney, S & Roycroft, N 2003 'Early enclosure at Balriggan, Co. Louth', *Archaeology Ireland*, Vol. 17, No. 2, 16–19.

Delaney, S & Walsh, F 2004 'Response to plectrum-shaped enclosures' [Letter], *Archaeology Ireland*, Vol. 18, No. 1, 6.

Doherty, C 2000 'Settlement in early Ireland: a review', *in* T Barry (ed.), *A History of Settlement in Ireland*, 50–80. Routledge, London and New York.

Donnelly, S, Donnelly, C & Murphy, E 1995 'The forgotten dead: the cillíní and disused burial grounds of Ballintoy, County Antrim', *Ulster Journal of Archaeology*, Vol. 58, 109–13.

Edwards, N 1990 *The Archaeology of Early Medieval Ireland*. Batsford, London.

Eogan, G 1991 'Irish antiquities of the Bronze Age, Iron Age and Early Christian periods in the National Museum of Denmark', *Proceedings of the Royal Irish Academy*, Vol. 91C, 133–76.

Eogan, G 2000 'Life and living at Lagore', *in* A P Smyth (ed.), *Seanchas: studies in early and medieval Irish archaeology, history and literature in honour of Francis J. Byrne*, 64–82. Four Courts Press, Dublin.

Fanning, T 1981 'Excavation of an Early Christian cemetery and settlement at Reask, County Kerry', *Proceedings of the Royal Irish Academy*, Vol. 81C, 67–172.

Farwell, D E & Molleson, T I 1993 *Excavations at Poundbury 1966–80 Vol. II: the cemeteries*. Dorset Natural History and Archaeology Society Monograph Series No. 11. Dorset Natural History and Archaeology Society, Dorset.

Feehan, J (ed.) 1983 *Laois: an environmental history*. Ballykilcavan Press, Stradbally.

Fibiger, L 2005 'Minor ailments, furious fights and deadly diseases: investigating life in Johnstown, County Meath, AD 400–1700', *in* J O'Sullivan & M Stanley (eds), 99–110.

Galloway, A 1997 'The process of decomposition: a model from the Arizona–Sonoran Desert', *in* W D Haglund & M H Sorg (eds), 139–50.

Gill-King, H 1997 'Chemical and ultrastructural aspects of decomposition', *in* W D Haglund & M H Sorg (eds), 93–108.

Gordon, D H 1953 'Fire and the sword: the technique of destruction', *Antiquity*, Vol. 27, No. 107, 149–52.

Gowen, M & Halpin, E 1992 'A Neolithic house at Newtown', *Archaeology Ireland*, Vol. 6, No. 2, 156.

Haglund, W D & Sorg, M H (eds) 1997 *Forensic Taphonomy: the postmortem fate of human remains*. CRC Press, Boca Raton, Florida, USA.

Haglund, W D & Sorg, M H (eds) 2002 *Advances in Forensic Taphonomy: method, theory, and archaeological perspectives*. CRC Press, Boca Raton, Florida, USA.

Hamlin, A & Foley, C 1983 'A women's graveyard at Carrickmore, Co. Tyrone, and the separate burial of women', *Ulster Journal of Archaeology*, Vol. 46, 41–6.

Hodkinson, B 1994 'Excavations at Cormac's Chapel, Cashel, 1992 and 1993: a preliminary statement', *Tipperary Historical Journal*, 1994, 167–74.

Hull, G & Taylor, K 2005 'Archaeology on the route of the Ennis Bypass', *The Other Clare*, Vol. 29, 35–41.

Kelly, F 1998 *Early Irish Farming*. Early Irish Law Series 4. Dublin Institute for Advanced Studies, Dublin.

Knox, H T 1907 'Notes on gig-mills and drying kilns near Ballyhaunis, County Mayo', *Proceedings of the Royal Irish Academy*, Vol. 2C, 264–75.

Leigh Fry, S 1999 *Burial in Medieval Ireland, 900–1500: a review of the written sources*. Four Courts Press, Dublin.

Limbert, D 1996 'Irish ringforts: a review of their origins', *Archaeological Journal*, Vol. 153, 243–89.

Lynn, C J 1987 'Deer Park Farms, Glenarm, County Antrim', *Archaeology Ireland*, Vol. 1, No. 1, 11–15.

MacDonagh, M 2005 'Valley bottom and hilltop: 6,000 years of settlement along the route of the N4 Sligo Inner Relief Road', *in* J O'Sullivan & M Stanley (eds), 9–23.

Mallory, J P & McNeill, T E 1991 *The Archaeology of Ulster: from colonization to plantation.* Institute of Irish Studies, Belfast.

Monk, M A 1986 'Evidence from macroscopic plant remains for crop husbandry in prehistoric and early historic Ireland: a review', *Journal of Irish Archaeology*, Vol. 3, 31–6.

Monk, M A 1998 'Early medieval secular and ecclesiastical settlement in Munster', *in* M A Monk & J Sheehan (eds), *Early Medieval Munster: archaeology, history and society,* 33–52. Cork University Press, Cork.

Moog, B 1994 *The Horizontal Watermill: history and technique of the first prime mover.* International Molinological Society, The Hague.

National Roads Authority 2005a *Guidelines for the Assessment of Archaeological Heritage Impacts of National Road Schemes.* National Roads Authority, Dublin.

National Roads Authority 2005b *Guidelines for the Assessment of Architectural Heritage Impacts of National Road Schemes.* National Roads Authority, Dublin.

National Roads Authority 2005c *Guidelines for the Testing and Mitigation of the Wetland Archaeological Heritage for National Road Schemes.* National Roads Authority, Dublin.

National Roads Authority and the Department of Arts, Heritage, Gaeltacht and the Islands 2000 *Code of Practice between the NRA and the Minister for Arts, Heritage, Gaeltacht and the Islands.* NRA and DAHGI, Dublin.

O'Brien, E 1999 *Post-Roman Britain to Anglo-Saxon England: burial practices reviewed.* British Archaeological Reports, British Series 289. Oxford.

O'Brien, R & Russell, I 2005 'The Hiberno-Scandinavian site of Woodstown 6, County Waterford', *in* J O'Sullivan & M Stanley (eds), 111–24.

O'Dowd, P 1998 'Leachta cuimhne or funerary cairns of Wormhole, Moycullen, Co. Galway', *Journal of the Galway Archaeological and Historical Society*, Vol. 50, 202–9.

Ó Drisceoil, C 2002 'Site 1, Coolfore', *in* I Bennett (ed.), *Excavations 2000: summary accounts of archaeological excavations in Ireland,* 214–15. Wordwell, Bray.

O'Kelly, M J 1951 'An Early Bronze Age ring-fort at Carrigillihy, Co. Cork', *Journal of the Cork Historical and Archaeological Society,* Vol. 56, 69–86.

O'Rahilly, T F 1946 *Early Irish History and Mythology* [1999 reprint]. School of Celtic Studies, Dublin.

Ó Ríordáin, S P 1949 'Lough Gur excavations: Carraig Aille and the Spectacles', *Proceedings of the Royal Irish Academy,* Vol. 52C, 39–111.

Orpen, G H 1911 *Ireland under the Normans, Vols I–II.* Clarendon Press, Oxford.

Orpen, G H 1921 'The Earldom of Ulster', *Journal of the Royal Society of Antiquaries of Ireland,* Vol. 50, 68–76.

O'Sullivan, J & Ó Carragáin, T in press *Inishmurray, County Sligo, Vol. 1—Archaeological survey and excavations in an ecclesiastical landscape, 1997–2000.* Department of the Environment, Heritage & Local Government, Dublin.

O'Sullivan, J & Stanley, M (eds) 2005 *Recent Archaeological Discoveries on National Road Schemes 2004.* Archaeology and the National Roads Authority Monograph Series No. 2. National Roads Authority, Dublin.

Parker Pearson, M 1999 *The Archaeology of Death and Burial.* Sutton Publishing, Thrupp.

Reimer, P J, Baillie, M G L, Bard, E, et al. 2004 'IntCal04 terrestrial radiocarbon age calibration, 0–26 ka cal BP', *Radiocarbon*, Vol. 46, No. 3, 1029–58.

Rodriguez, W C, III 1997 'Decomposition of buried and submerged bodies', *in* W D Haglund & M H Sorg (eds), 459–67.

Roksandic, M 2002 'Position of skeletal remains as a key to understanding mortuary behavior', *in* W D Haglund & M H Sorg (eds), 99–117.

Roycroft, N 2005 'Around the bay on the Great North Road: the archaeology of the M1 Dundalk Western Bypass', *in* J O'Sullivan & M Stanley (eds), 65–82.

Rynne, C 2000 'Waterpower in medieval Ireland', *in* P Squatriti (ed.), *Working with Water in Medieval Europe*, 1–50. Brill Academic Publishers, Leiden.

Saul, J M & Saul, F P 2002 'Forensics, archaeology, and taphonomy: the symbiotic relationship', *in* W D Haglund & M H Sorg (eds), 71–97.

Schweitzer, H 2005 'Iron Age toe-rings from Rath, County Meath, on the N2 Finglas–Ashbourne Road Scheme', *in* J O'Sullivan & M Stanley (eds), 93–8.

Stevanovic, M 1997 'The age of clay: the social dynamics of house destruction', *Journal of Anthropological Archaeology*, Vol. 16, 334–95.

Stout, M 1997 *The Irish Ringfort*. Four Courts Press, Dublin.

Stout, M 2000 'Early Christian Ireland: settlement and environment', *in* T Barry (ed.), *A History of Settlement in Ireland*, 81–109. Routledge, London.

Stout, M 2003 'Ringforts', *in* B Lalor (ed.), *The Encyclopaedia of Ireland*, 931. Gill & Macmillan, Dublin.

Stuiver, M, Reimer, P J, Bard, E, et al. 1998 'IntCal98 Radiocarbon Age Calibration, 24,000–0 cal BP', *Radiocarbon*, Vol. 40, No. 3, 1041–83.

Stuiver, M, Reimer, P J & Reimer, R W 2005 *CALIB 5.0*. http://www.calib.qub.ac.uk/calib/

Walsh, F & Harrison, J 2003 'Early medieval enclosure at Killickaweeny, Co. Kildare', *Archaeology Ireland*, Vol. 17, No. 1, 33–6.

Warner, R 1979 'The Irish souterrains and their background', *in* H Crawford (ed.), *Subterranean Britain*, 100–44. A & C Black, London.

Warner, R 1980 'Irish souterrains: later Iron Age refuges', *Archaeologia Atlantica*, Vol. 3, 81–99.

Warner, R & Meighan, I G 1994 'Dating Irish glass beads through chemical analysis', *in* D Ó Corráin (ed.), *Irish Antiquity*, 52–66. Four Courts Press, Dublin.

Wheeler, R E M 1943 *Maiden Castle, Dorset*. Reports of the Research Committee of the Society of Antiquaries of London, No. 12.

White Marshall, J & Rourke, G D 2000 *High Island: an island monastery in the Atlantic*. Town and Country House, Dublin.

Seminar programme

Introduction
Fred Barry
Chief Executive, National Roads Authority

A Neolithic settlement at Monanny, Co. Monaghan
Fintan Walsh
Excavation Director, Irish Archaeological Consultancy Ltd

Archaeological discoveries from the N2 Finglas–Ashbourne Road Scheme Project
Maria FitzGerald
Project Archaeologist, Meath County Council National Roads Design Office

Through the mill—the excavation of significant early medieval settlement at Raystown, County Meath, on the N2 road realignment
Matthew Seaver
Excavation Director, Cultural Resource Development Services Ltd

Excavation of a ringfort at Leggetsrath West, Kilkenny
Anne-Marie Lennon
Excavation Director, Archaeological Consultancy Services Ltd

Excavation of a children's burial ground at Tonybaun, Co. Mayo
Joanna Nolan
Excavation Director, Mayo County Council

Excavation of an early medieval vertical watermill at Killoteran, Co. Waterford
Donald Murphy
Excavation Director, Archaeological Consultancy Services Ltd

Aerial survey—a method of investigation for archaeological studies at the EIS stage of the planning process
Lisa Courtney
Senior Archaeologist, Margaret Gowen & Co. Ltd

Excavation of a 'plectrum-shaped' enclosure at Newtown, Co. Limerick
Frank Coyne
Excavation Director, Aegis Archaeology Ltd

Excavation of a souterrain at Tateetra, Dundalk, Co. Louth
Avril Hayes
Excavation Director, Aegis Archaeology Ltd

The excavation of an early church and burial site at Ballykilmore, Co. Westmeath
John Channing
Excavation Director
and
Patrick Randolph-Quinney
Osteoarchaeologist, Valerie J Keeley Ltd

Archaeology and the National Roads Authority: five years on
Dáire O'Rourke
Senior Archaeologist, National Roads Authority

Glossary

Alluvium Fine-grained, well-sorted soils deposited by rivers.

Archaeometallurgy The study of the archaeology of metal production.

Artefact Any portable object that has been used, modified or manufactured by humans.

Assemblage All of the artefacts found at a site, including the sum of all sub-assemblages at the site.

Bailey Fortified enclosed courtyard or ward surrounding or attached to a medieval castle. Also a fortified earthwork enclosure attached to a motte (see motte and bailey).

Barrow An earthen burial mound, generally dating to the Bronze Age and Iron Age.

Bronze Age The period c. 2400–600 BC that succeeded the Neolithic period and saw the introduction of bronze for tools and weapons.

Burnt mound A mound of burnt stones that can be found in isolation or in association with a *fulacht fiadh* (see below).

Cairn A mound of stones.

Capstone A slab or block of stone forming the top of a burial cist or the roof of a chambered tomb or souterrain.

Carinated/carination A break in the profile of a pottery vessel, which forms a keel or ridge, usually marking the junction of the body with the neck.

Causewayed enclosure A Neolithic enclosure with circuits of ditch interrupted by causeways. An embankment or palisade stood within the ditch.

Chert A flint-like material, usually black or dark brown, that is a form of very fine, crystalline silica.

Collared Urn A type of Bronze Age pottery vessel with a flat base, conical body and heavy overhanging rim or collar.

Context A generic term for the smallest identifiable stratigraphic unit recognised in an excavation.

Cordoned Urn A type of Middle Bronze Age pottery probably derived from Collared Urns (see above). The outer face is decorated with applied cordons or raised ribs.

Crannóg A defended settlement, mainly dating from the early medieval period, built on an artificial, or artificially enlarged, island.

Cremation The practice of burning the dead. In prehistory the ashes were commonly placed in a pottery vessel and buried in a pit.

Cropmarks Patterns or variations in the colour or growth rates of pasture or planted crops; these often relate to buried archaeological features.

Debitage Detached pieces of stone from larger stone cores that are discarded during the process of stone tool production.

Dendrochronology A dating method based on the study of tree-rings as a means of providing precise calendar dates.

Drystone walling Walls constructed of stone without the use of mortar.

Enclosure A piece of ground surrounded by a boundary such as a wall, bank or ditch.

Encrusted Urn A Bronze Age pottery vessel with heavy applied decoration in horizontal and vertical bands around the upper portion of the body.

Environmental Impact Assessment The process for anticipating the effects on the environment caused by a development. An Environmental Impact Statement is the document produced as a result of that process.

Environmental Impact Statement See Environmental Impact Assessment, above.

Faience Blue artificial glass-like material made from baked siliceous clay.

Feature This term refers to any component of an archaeological site such as a post-hole, pit, wall, ditch or any deposit that may have accumulated on the site.

Fibula A decorative brooch of safety-pin form to fasten a cloak or other garment.

Flint A hard, brittle siliceous rock with conchoidal fracturing properties that is highly suitable for the manufacture of edged tools.

Food Vessel Heavily decorated biconical or bowl-shaped Early Bronze Age pot, mainly associated with cremation burials.

Fulacht fiadh A site, generally dating from the Bronze Age, consisting of a horseshoe-shaped mound of burnt stones, a hearth(s) and a trough(s). These sites were used to heat water for a variety of possible purposes. Also known as ancient cooking places.

Geophysical survey Methods of exploring below the surface of the ground by measuring anomalies in the soil's magnetic susceptibility, electrical resistivity and other properties capable of being detected by instruments.

Hammerstone A rock used to detach smaller fragments of stone from a larger core during the production of stone tools, or any other percussive process.

Henge A more or less circular enclosure, normally with the bank outside the ditch and often enclosing a circle of stones.

Hone stone A whetstone for sharpening edged tools.

Infield A field located close to a farmhouse, comprising arable and manured land kept continually under crop.

Inhumation The name given to the burial custom by which the body was laid in a grave.

Iron Age Final period of prehistory, beginning around 600 BC. Iron superseded bronze for the manufacture of tools and weapons in this period.

La Tène The site of an Iron Age votive deposit of metal artefacts, some bearing distinctive curvilinear decoration, at Lake Neuchâtel, Switzerland. La Tène has given its name to La Tène art and to the second period of the European Iron Age.

Lithics General archaeological term applied to all collections of stone tools, working debris and raw materials.

Loom-weight A weight used to weigh down the threads (known as warps) that run lengthways on a loom.

Medieval Period succeeding the Iron Age, in Ireland from the advent of Christianity in the fifth century up to the 16th century AD.

Megalith A large stone used in the construction of prehistoric tombs, stone circles and stone alignments.

Mesolithic The Middle Stone Age, c. 7000–4000 BC, when Ireland was first settled by early hunters and foragers.

Metalling/metalled surface The hard-packed surface of a road, track or street, comprising layers of gravel and stone.

Microlith A very small stone tool, characteristic of the Early Mesolithic period, which is generally thought to have been hafted for use (e.g. as barbs and tips of arrows).

Monitoring The presence of an archaeologist during development works, such as topsoil removal, to identify and record archaeological deposits, features or objects.

Motte A Norman fortification consisting of a round mound, flattened on top, and thought to have been surmounted by a wooden tower or palisade.

Motte and bailey A Norman military stronghold comprising a motte, surrounded by a ditch, with an adjoining separately defined enclosure known as a bailey.

Neolithic The Late Stone Age, c. 4000–2400 BC, characterised by the beginnings of farming.

Osteology/Osteoarchaeology A branch of archaeology that deals with the study and analysis of human and animal skeletal remains.

Palaeoenvironment An ancient or past environment.

Palisade A stake-built or post-built defensive barrier, often positioned on top of an embankment or rampart.

Porcellanite A type of metamorphic rock used in the manufacture of stone axes.

Post-excavation A general term applied to those analytical and reporting tasks to be undertaken following the fieldwork stage of an archaeological project.

Post-hole The void or soil-filled hole where a post once stood.

Post-medieval The period after the medieval period, often taken to be the period after the dissolution of the monasteries in the mid-16th century.

Prehistoric Any period for which there is no contemporary documentary evidence.

Quern-stone A large stone used for grinding grain into flour.

Radiocarbon dating A dating method that measures the decay of the radioactive isotope Carbon 14, which is present in all organic material.

Rath A circular earthen enclosure, otherwise known as a ringfort.

Record of Monuments and Places A list of archaeological sites with accompanying maps recorded on a county-by-county basis by the State. Inclusion in the list affords archaeological sites certain legal protections.

Revetment Facing of hard, solid material given to a structure built with softer, less stable material to retain and support it.

Ring-ditch A small circular enclosure defined by a ring-shaped ditch, which is often associated with prehistoric burials. Many have been discovered to be ploughed-out barrows (see above).

Ringfort A defended farmstead, mainly dating from between the seventh and ninth centuries AD, enclosed by one or more concentric earthworks comprising a bank and outer ditch.

Ring-pin Early medieval dress-fastener, usually of copper-alloy, with a swivel ring inserted through a perforation in the pin.

Roadtake The land area to be occupied by a proposed road.

Scraper Stone tool comprising a round or horseshoe-shaped flake deliberately shaped to provide a working edge.

Site A term used to refer to places of archaeological interest or potential.

Slag Partly vitrified waste material from the smelting of a metal ore or glass-making.

Souterrain A long, narrow, stone-walled subterranean gallery, usually with a slab roof. Some have small chambers off the main passage.

Standing stone A block or slab of stone set upright as a marker, dating mainly from the Neolithic and Bronze Age.

Stone alignment/row A line of upright stones set at intervals along an axis. They are common from the later Neolithic period and Bronze Age.

Stratigraphy The laying down of layers one above the other. A succession of layers should provide a relative chronological sequence for the events it represents or the objects it contains.

Test excavation A limited form of archaeological excavation where the purpose is to establish the nature, extent, significance and, if possible, the date of archaeological deposits and features.

Tower house Fortified residence commonly built from the 15th century through to the 17th century.

Trial trench See test excavation, above.

Vase Urn A type of Bronze Age pottery consisting of small hand-made, well-decorated vases.

Vertical mill A type of mill with a vertical wheel, driven by water directed onto paddles from below or from above.

Viking (*Vikingur*) Scandinavian word for seafaring raiders from Norway, Sweden and Denmark who ravaged the coasts of Europe from the seventh century AD onwards.

Directory of NRA Archaeologists and local authority Project Archaeologists

NRA Archaeologists

Dáire O'Rourke   Senior Archaeologist   *NRA Dublin*
National Roads Authority
St Martin's House
Waterloo Road
Dublin 4
telephone 01 6602511
e-mail dorourke@nra.ie

Róisín Barton-Murray   Archaeologist   *NRA Dublin*
National Roads Authority
St Martin's House
Waterloo Road
Dublin 4
telephone 01 6602511
e-mail rbarton@nra.ie

Michael Stanley   Assistant Archaeologist   *NRA Dublin*
National Roads Authority
St Martin's House
Waterloo Road
Dublin 4
telephone 01 6602511
e-mail mstanley@nra.ie

Local authority Project Archaeologists

Ken Hanley   National Roads Design Office   *Cork County Council*
Cork County Council
Richmond
Glanmire
County Cork
telephone 021 4821046
e-mail ken.hanley@corkrdo.ie

Michael MacDonagh   National Roads Design Office   *Donegal County Council*
Donegal County Council
Public Services Centre
Drumlonagher
Donegal Town
County Donegal
telephone 074 9724505
e-mail michael.macdonagh@dnrdo.ie

Jerry O'Sullivan   National Roads Design Office   *Galway County Council*
Galway County Council
Corporate House
Ballybrit Business Park
Galway
telephone 091 735335
e-mail jerryosullivan@galwaycoco.ie

Sébastien Joubert   National Roads Design Office   *Kerry County Council*
Kerry County Council
The Island Centre
Castleisland
County Kerry
telephone 066 7142444
e-mail sjouber@kerrycoco.ie

Sylvia Desmond   National Roads Design Office   *Kildare County Council*
Kildare County Council
Maudlins
Naas
County Kildare
telephone 045 898199
e-mail sdesmond@kildarenrdo.com

Noel Dunne   National Roads Design Office   *Kildare County Council*
Kildare County Council
Maudlins
Naas
County Kildare
telephone 045 898199
e-mail ndunne@kildarenrdo.com

Celie O Rahilly   Mid West National Road   *Limerick County Council*
Design Office
Limerick County Council
Mungret College
County Limerick
telephone 061 227382
e-mail corahilly@midwestroads.ie

Gerry Walsh   National Roads Design Office   *Mayo County Council*
Mayo County Council
Glenparke House
The Mall
Castlebar
County Mayo
telephone 094 9038131
e-mail gwalsh@regdesign.com

Mary Deevy	National Roads Design Office Meath County Council Navan Enterprise Centre Trim Road Navan County Meath telephone 046 9075033 e-mail mdeevy@meathcoco.ie	*Meath County Council*
Niall Roycroft	National Roads Design Office Meath County Council Navan Enterprise Centre Trim Road Navan County Meath telephone 046 9075033 e-mail nroycroft@meathcoco.ie	*Meath County Council*
Maria FitzGerald	National Roads Design Office Meath County Council Navan Enterprise Centre Trim Road Navan County Meath telephone 046 9075033 e-mail mfitzgerald@meathcoco.ie	*Meath County Council*
James Eogan	Tramore House Regional Design Office Waterford County Council Pond Road, Tramore County Waterford telephone 051 390130 e-mail jeogan@thrdo.com	*Waterford County Council*
Richard O'Brien	Tramore House Regional Design Office Waterford County Council Pond Road Tramore County Waterford telephone 051 390130 e-mail robrien@thrdo.com	*Waterford County Council*
Rónán Swan	National Roads Design Office Westmeath County Council Cullenbeg, Mullingar County Westmeath telephone 044 34250 e-mail rswan@wccprojectoffice.ie	*Westmeath County Council*

Assistant Project Archaeologists

Caroline Healy   National Roads Design Office   *Cork County Council*
Cork County Council
Richmond
Glanmire
County Cork
telephone 021 4821046
e-mail chealy@corkrdo.ie

Gráinne Leamy   National Roads Design Office   *Donegal County Council*
Donegal County Council
Public Services Centre
Drumlonagher
Donegal Town
County Donegal
telephone 074 9724505
e-mail grainne.leamy@dnrdo.ie

Martin Jones   National Roads Design Office   *Galway County Council*
Galway County Council,
Corporate House
Ballybrit Business Park
Galway
telephone 091 735333
e-mail mjones@galwaycoco.ie

Elspeth Logan   National Roads Design Office   *Kildare County Council*
Kildare County Council
Maudlins, Naas
County Kildare
telephone 045 898199
e-mail elogan@kildarenrdo.com

Clare Crowley   National Roads Design Office   *Meath County Council*
Meath County Council
Navan Enterprise Centre
Trim Road, Navan
County Meath
telephone 046 9075033
e-mail ccrowley@meathcoco.ie

Freya Smith   Tramore House   *Waterford County Council*
Regional Design Office
Waterford County Council
Pond Road
Tramore
County Waterford
telephone 051 390130
e-mail fsmith@thrdo.com

Bernice Kelly   Tramore House   *Waterford County Council*
                     Regional Design Office
                     Waterford County Council
                     Pond Road
                     Tramore
                     County Waterford
                     telephone 051 390130
                     e-mail bkelly@thrdo.com

Mairead McLaughlin   Tramore House   *Waterford County Council*
                     Regional Design Office
                     Waterford County Council
                     Pond Road
                     Tramore
                     County Waterford
                     telephone 051 390130
                     e-mail mmclaughlin@thrdo.com

Orlaith Egan   National Roads Design Office   *Westmeath County Council*
                     Westmeath County Council
                     Cullenbeg
                     Mullingar
                     County Westmeath
                     telephone 044 34250
                     e-mail oegan@wccprojectoffice.ie